Dales Way

Ilkley to Bowness-on-Windermere

Jacquetta Megarry
& Peter Stott

Rucksack Readers

Dales Way

Revised edition published in 2026, partly drawing on updated text from a previous edition (2011) with new mapping, fresh photos and thoroughly revised text

Rucksack Readers, 6 Old Church Lane, Edinburgh EH15 3PX

Phone +44/0 131 661 0262

Website *www.rucsacs.com*

Email *info@rucsacs.com*

Text, design and layout © Rucksack Readers 2026; photos © Rucksack Readers and licensors, see page 87.

Mapping was created specially for this book © copyright Rucksack Readers 2026 by Lovell Johns. It contains Ordnance Survey data © Crown copyright and database right 2026 supplemented with original fieldwork by the authors.

The rights of Jacquetta Megarry and Peter Stott to be identified as the authors of this work have been asserted by them in accordance with the Copyright, Designs and Patents Act 1988.

All rights reserved. No part of this publication may be reproduced, stored in a retrieval system, or transmitted in any form or by any means (electronic, mechanical, photocopying, recording or otherwise) without prior permission in writing from the publisher.

ISBN 978-1-913817-33-6

British Library Cataloguing in Publication Data: a catalogue record for this book is available from the British Library.

Design and illustrations by Ian Clydesdale (ian@clydesdale.scot)

Printed on rainproof, biodegradable paper in Czechia via Akcent Media of St Neots, UK

Publisher's note

All information was checked prior to publication. However, changes are inevitable: take local advice and look out for waymarkers and other signage e.g. for diversions. Check two websites before setting out: *www.dalesway.org* and *www.rucsacs.com/books/daw*

Some parts of the Path may be wet underfoot, others are exposed and remote, and the weather in northern England is unpredictable year-round. You are responsible for your own safety, and for ensuring that your clothing, food and equipment are suited to your needs. The publisher cannot accept any liability for any ill-health, accident or loss arising directly or indirectly from reading this book.

Feedback is welcome and will be rewarded.

We are grateful to readers for comments and suggestions. All feedback will be followed up, and readers whose comments lead to changes will be entitled to claim a free book. Please send emails to *info@rucsacs.com*.

Contents

Introduction   4

Part 1

1   Planning and preparation
      Route options   5
      How long will it take?   6
      Season and weather   8
      Gradients and profile   8
      Terrain   9
      Waymarkers and navigation   10
      Responsible walking and livestock   11
      Pronunciation, dogs   12
      Safety and emergencies   13
      Accommodation and refreshments   14
      Travel planning   17
      Local words and placenames   18
      Packing checklist   19

Part 2

2·1   Geology and scenery   20
2·2   Mining, quarrying and the railways   22
2·3   Farming, tourism and conservation   24
2·4   Habitats and wildlife   26
2·5   The religious heritage   30

Part 3

3·1   Link Routes to Ilkley   33
      Ilkley   34
3·2   Ilkley to Burnsall   36
3·3   Burnsall to Buckden   43
3·4   Buckden to Cowgill   49
3·5   Cowgill to Sedbergh   58
      Dent village and Dentdale   61
      Sedbergh   64
3·6   Sedbergh to Burneside   66
3·7   Burneside to Bowness   73
      Bowness-on-Windermere   80

Part 4

      Watershed Alternatives   81

Reference material   86
Index   88

Introduction

The Dales Way connects the former spa town of Ilkley to the popular resort of Bowness-on-Windermere in the Lake District. Over your 80-mile journey, you will pass through two National Parks, and enjoy rural walking with some panoramic views.

The Way was devised in 1968 as a valley walk from Ilkley to Crook of Lune at the north-western edge of Yorkshire's then county of West Riding. Later, it was extended over undulating pastures to the Lake District, an iconic destination for generations of enthusiastic walkers and the birthplace of English romantic literature.

Most of the main Way lies below the 300 m (1000 feet) contour and it has no craggy terrain nor even many steep gradients. Much of it runs on gentle, grassy riverside paths, visiting attractive stone villages in sheltered valleys. Nonetheless, you enjoy extensive views of the Pennines, Howgills and Lake District fells and distant views of Yorkshire's Three Peaks.

Transport links at each end are good, with frequent trains and buses to Leeds and Manchester, both with international airports. A bus service runs parallel to the Way between Ilkley and Buckden. The dramatic Settle-Carlisle railway cuts through the high ground in the middle, with many impressive viaducts. There's also the option to ride between two of its most remarkable stations, at Ribblehead and Dent.

The walk has its spiritual moments, passing the delicate ruins of the 12th century Augustinian Bolton Priory at its riverside beauty spot. The Quaker heritage is visible both at Farfield Meetinghouse and around Sedbergh: see page 32. The peaceful valleys of the Wharfe, Dee and Lune host a range of wildlife against a backdrop of sheep farming. And Bowness makes a fitting lakeside destination.

We recommend you to follow the traditional direction, from Ilkley to Bowness. It feels deeply appropriate to walk from the dales to the lakes. Starting from a former industrial area you pass through classic Dales scenery with scattered farms, barns and drystone walls to reach England's largest lake at journey's end.

Despite its great popularity with walkers, the Dales Way has no official status: it's a people's path, rather than a National Trail. For this reason, we encourage you to join the Dales Way Association and to benefit from its resources: see page 86.

River Wharfe, framed by chestnut trees

1 Planning and preparation

The Dales Way uses public footpaths and bridleways, permissive paths, farm tracks, old drove roads, byways and public roads. You will cross a living, working landscape that includes river valleys, meadows, woodland, upland pastures and rough moorland. Some sections of the Way are heavily used, well maintained and the route is obvious. Elsewhere, paths may be faint or vanishing, and navigation may demand your careful attention, including alertness to waymarkers of different kinds: see page 10.

Subject to that, this route makes a good choice as your first long-distance walk if you prepare for it suitably. The most important decisions are your route options and how many days to allow for your itinerary: see pages 6-7. In addition, consider footwear, fitness, rucksack and route-finding. For more about these, obtain our *Notes for novices:* see page 87.

The Way will reward you with inspiring scenery, fresh air and warm rural hospitality. The simplicity of style in the Dales combines well with the sleep-eat-walk rhythm of long-distance walking. There is plenty of space to enjoy the contrasts with city life, and opportunities to enjoy the no-nonsense attitude of those who work here. For a guide to pronunciation, and the meanings of local words and placenames, see pages 12 and 18.

Route options

First you need to decide which version of the Dales Way you intend to undertake. The Link Routes offer three options for walking to Ilkley from Bradford, Leeds or Harrogate, and are summarised on pages 33-4 and mapped in our map booklet at 1:40,000 see page 87. For a shorter warm-up, you could join the Bradford Link at Shipley Station: see page 33.

Watershed Alternatives

Several options were created by the created by the opening of a new section of Pennine Bridleway in 2011. We describe and map them fully on pages 81-85 but don't wait until Part 4 to consider the benefits of these options – in part or in full.

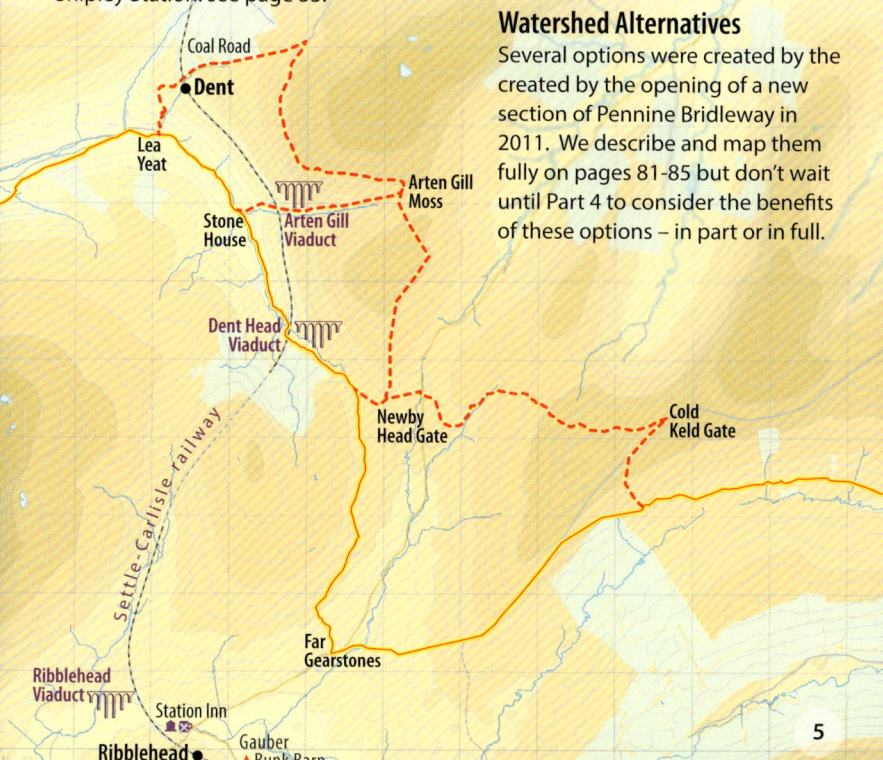

The 2024 landslip on the road below Dent Head Viaduct created a pressing reason to use at least the central section over Wold Fell: see pages 81-3. As we go to press in February 2026, that road was still closed to walkers, as well as vehicles: see **www.rucsacs.com/books/daw** for Route updates.

Many will prefer to leave the route sooner, at Cam Houses – thus saving 1·5 miles (2·4 km) of lower-level road walking, while enjoying better going underfoot and fine open views. And, instead of descending beside Artengill Beck, many will choose to continue their lofty walk around the shoulder of Great Knoutberry and descend to the dale past Dent Station to Cowgill. These Alternatives have great advantages, even when the road closure doesn't force you to take them. The best way to decide your preference is to read carefully our route descriptions on pages 51 to 55 and 81 to 85.

A final issue may seem to be about which direction: given that the prevailing weather systems come in from the south-west, might it be better to head east from Bowness and then south-east to Ilkley? And when walking from Cam Houses to Dent Head Viaduct, the views of the Three Peaks are behind you, so might it be more scenic if reversed? In practice, few people reverse the direction, and almost nobody does it this way first time around. We advise against it.

How long will it take?

Experienced walkers will already know roughly what daily distance they find comfortable, and will interpret the distance tables accordingly. Novices should beware of assuming they will walk at anything like the speeds they might attain on an urban pavement, with no serious obstacles, tricky terrain or severe gradients.

We measure the distance along the spine of the route at just under 80 miles (128 km), but you will see official signs at start and finish that mention both 81 and 82 miles. The truth is that you will walk much farther, probably at least 90 miles. The reasons include:

- getting to the start and returning from the finish of the route
- going offroute for accommodation and refreshments
- making diversions e.g. accidental backtracking and deliberate detours.

Factors that will reduce your average speed, probably more than you expect:

- brief pauses (e.g. to spot wildlife, take photos or enjoy the views)
- longer stops (e.g. to visit churches, Bolton Priory, have lunch)
- obstacles such as stream crossings, boggy terrain, territorial livestock and stiles.

Because the Dales Way doesn't feature extreme gradients or high altitude, many people underestimate its terrain. It has a large number of gates and stiles, and if the trail is busy they can become bottlenecks. Some gates can be tricky to unfasten and refasten, and most stiles take longer, especially tall ladder-stiles: see also page 9.

In this book, we present the main route in six sections but we regard six days as the bare minimum that a recreational walker should consider. Viewed as an endurance challenge, a few hardy souls may complete the Way in under 24 hours. However, if your goal is to have a fulfilling week, reconnect with Nature, enjoy the scenery and appreciate the heritage, then putting yourself under time pressure may be self-defeating.

The tables show three options for splitting the route so that walkers who want a soft bed and an evening meal each day can avoid excessive daily distances. Even so, note that the 6-day option involves a nearly 18-mile (29-km) day to which you must add the accommodation distance – negligible if you can get into the Shepherds Cottage, but an extra 3-mile round trip if you walk to Ribblehead. If 18 miles is more than you wish to walk in a day, see Table 1c for a neat workaround using the railway (that also circumvents any road closure).

Stone bench at Bowness

We believe that most readers will benefit from at least seven days: Table 1b shows the full Dales Way with the longest day now Burnsall to Hubberholme (15·1 miles), whilst no section in Table 1c exceeds 13·2 miles.

Your choice of itinerary will be affected by your plans for accommodation, taking account of budget and availability, as well as whether you prefer (or are obliged by road closure) to use the Watershed Alternatives: see pages 81-85. Note that both Tables 1a and 1b assume that you will follow the road below Dent Head Viaduct, whereas Table 1c reflects the slightly shorter route created by going from Cam Houses Via Arten Gill Moss to descend the Coal Road past Dent Station.

Three options for spreading the distance over six or seven days

Table 1a (6 days)	miles	km	Table 1b (7 days)	miles	km	Table 1c (7 days)	miles	km
Ilkley			Ilkley			Ilkley		
	13·2	21·2		13·2	21·2		13·2	21·2
Burnsall			Burnsall			Burnsall		
	13·8	22·2		15·1	24·3		9·5	15·3
Buckden			Hubberholme			Kettlewell		
	17·7	28·5		11·3	18·2		12·1	19·5
Cowgill *			Far Gearstones			Swarthghyll		
	12·7	20·4		9·2	14·8		9·2	14·8
Sedbergh *			Dent			Cowgill #		
	12·3	19·8		9·6	15·4		12·7	20·4
Burneside			Branthwaite			Sedbergh *		
	9·9	15·9		11·3	18·2		12·3	19·8
Bowness			Burneside			Burneside		
				9·9	15·9		9·9	15·9
			Bowness			Bowness		
Total	79·6	128·1	Total	79·6	128·1	Total	78·9	127·0

All distances are measured along the spine of the route and exclude detours to accommodation.

* Distances to Cowgill are measured to Lea Yeat Bridge, and Sedbergh is taken to mean Lincoln's Inn Bridge (mile 57·4), although you approach the town more closely at Millthrop Bridge (mile 53·8)

\# This distance uses the Watershed Alternatives from Cam Houses to Lea Yeat (with possible train to Ribblehead from Dent Station)

Season and weather

In theory, you can walk the Way in any month. If you live locally, you can seize upon a few days of brilliant winter weather at short notice. Walkers from further afield must book accommodation well ahead (unless relying on camping), and generally should avoid November-March. Accommodation will be harder to find, and conditions underfoot can be sodden. Spring comes late to the higher ground, with the best months being May to September. Always check the forecast before setting out: see the foot of page 86.

With a latitude of about 54° N, daylight hours in northern England range from about 18 in late June to barely 8 in late December. Between November and January, avoid attempting long daily distances. At any time between October and March try to set out at first light and carry a head-torch.

Average monthly rainfall for Ilkley is shown in the graph below. Windermere has 51% more rainfall than Ilkley, with the difference greater in winter months. At any time of year, the short-term effects of heavy recent rainfall can include flooding and even landslip. Average daily temperatures rise to 14-15 °C from June to September and drop to 4-5 °C from November to March.

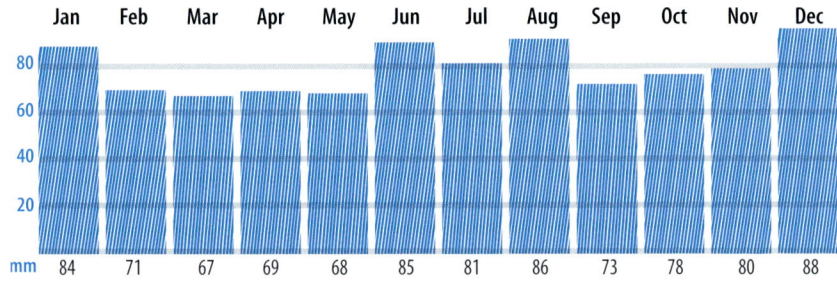

Rainfall in mm in Ilkley (c. 1991-2000) courtesy of *climate-data.org*

Gradients and profile

The profile below shows the main Dales Way in solid red and the Watershed Alternative as a pecked line above. The main route reaches its maximum height 525 m (1720 ft) on Cam High Road and otherwise mostly stays below 400 m (1310 ft), with much of the route confined to fairly sheltered dales. Gradients are seldom severe, and generally the greatest constraints on your speed are more likely to be from terrain and obstacles.

Notice, however, that although the Watershed Alternatives go higher than the main Way, the difference is only 45 metres and the main route has a greater loss of altitude after its high point. The Alternatives involve only a small extra altitude, more than offset by the easier, better-drained terrain.

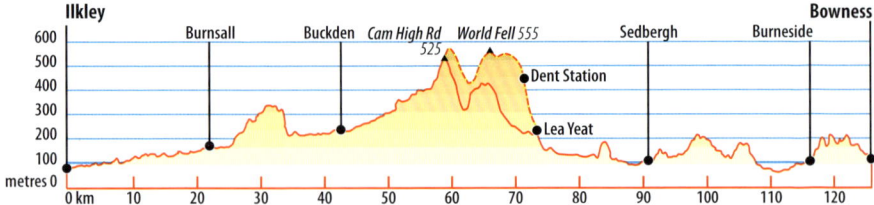

Terrain

Gates and stiles are frequent in some sections, and they will affect your average pace surprisingly. Suppose you average 4 km per hour (that's 2·5 mph) without stiles: that's realistic for brisk walking over mixed terrain with no rest stops. At that rate, each km takes you 15 minutes. If the next km includes 5 stiles and you take an average of one minute to cross each one, that 1 km will now take 20 minutes instead of 15. This reduces your average speed from 4 to 3 kph. (In case you think five stiles per km is far-fetched, see page 48, bullet 2 about the approach to Kettlewell.)

The main Way features an astonishing range of stiles: some are very easy to cross but others may hold you up significantly. We illustrate some varieties in the collage below, together with some other obstacles to progress.

Waymarkers and navigation

Unlike England's National Trails, the Dales Way is not government-funded. As a result, waymarking is less consistent, with a range of discs and fingerposts bearing a 'Dales Way' legend or icon. The collage illustrates the variety as photographed in October 2025, but styles may vary over the years. Parts of the route require intricate navigation and you are strongly advised to keep checking your position against our mapping. Keeping our map booklet in a handy pocket makes this easy to do.

Don't be tempted to follow other walkers: they may be on a completely different walk, or they may have mistakenly missed a turning. If in real doubt about navigation, by all means talk to other walkers, or to a local resident if you see one. Generally, it's safest to backtrack to wherever you were last certain you were on the Way. Do not cut across fields or risk any damage to crops, gates or walls.

Don't expect reassurance at every stile, gate or junction. Often a Public Footpath disc, footpath fingerpost or plain arrow is all the help you will get. But beware: sometimes such arrows are pointing out an unrelated footpath that will take you off the Way.

Even the official discs with logos look very different according to which National Park issued them: see the discs above. The LDNP discs are often blue but other types of marker appear. And if you are following the Watershed Alternative from Cam Houses, you should be following Pennine Bridleway markers at first.

Responsible walking and livestock

Always respect the land and its residents. Co-operation with farmers and other landowners improves relations between those who visit the countryside and those who live and work there. Keep to the footpath, especially in hay meadows, which yield a vitally important crop.

Always close and fasten gates after passing through, unless a farmer has deliberately left a gate open. Litter is unsightly, as well as being potentially lethal to farm animals and wildlife. Whatever you carry in, please carry out, and dispose of it properly. If you see a piece of litter that somebody else dropped, consider if you could pick it up. This would improve the route for everybody, and set a splendid example.

Lambing takes place between March and June in the Dales: never disturb pregnant ewes, nor approach young lambs. Cattle can be fiercely protective of their young: give them a wide berth, especially if calves are nearby. What should you do if you find cattle blocking your path? The photo below was taken near Addingham while researching this book: the Dales Way marker* is visible at the step-stile. The cattle point-blank refused to give way to me, no matter how much noise I made or how hard I tried to make myself look larger.

Not wishing to risk forcing my way, I decided to take photos, bide my time and wait until another couple of walkers came along. Having enlisted their help, the three of us made enough noise to cause the cattle to move aside, slowly and calmly, and we all slipped through the stile. This incident was a valuable reminder that sometimes you will face unexpected delays, and your itinerary must allow for this.

Countryside Code

Respect everyone
- be considerate to those living in, working in and enjoying the countryside
- leave gates and property as you find them
- do not block access to gateways or driveways when parking
- be nice, say hello, share the space
- follow local signs and keep to marked paths unless wider access is available

Protect the environment
- take your litter home – leave no trace of your visit
- do not light fires and only have BBQs where signs say you can
- always keep dogs under control and in sight
- dog poo – bag it and bin it – any public waste bin will do
- care for nature – do not cause damage or disturbance

Enjoy the outdoors
- check your route and local conditions
- plan your adventure – know what to expect and what you can do
- enjoy your visit, have fun, make a memory

Cattle blocking access to the step-stile

Pronunciation

If you haven't visited this area before, you may be unsure about how to pronounce some placenames:

Appletreewick	**app** trick	Hubberholme	**hub** er um
Blea Moor	**blee** moor	Lea Yeat	lee **yate** (rhymes with gate)
Burneside	**burn** ee side	Oughtershaw	**outa** shaw
Conistone	**con** is tun	Sedbergh	**sed** ber

Dogs

Think carefully before bringing a dog. Visiting dogs are unwelcome in sheep country, particularly in the lambing season. They must be kept on a short lead (2 m or less) near farm animals, and they are not permitted on some areas of Access Land, lest they disturb ground-nesting birds. Always clean up after your dog if it soils the path, and dispose of the poo responsibly.

Several practical issues arise for walkers with dogs. Many places where you might wish to eat or sleep will not allow your dog indoors. Some B&Bs accept dogs with extra cleaning charges, but more exclude dogs: check carefully before booking. Depending on the policies of pubs and cafés, you may be better to carry the food and drink that you and your dog need.

The number of stiles along the Way demands a lot of time and energy from most dogs; depending on the dog's weight and attitude, a tall ladder-stile may present a serious obstacle. Ensure that your dog is fit enough to manage the distances, and take care of his feet.

Having a dog with you may exacerbate livestock issues. It isn't just a matter of ensuring that the dog doesn't disturb farm animals: it's also vital to know what to do if the dog's presence spooks cattle and thus puts your own safety at risk. The National Farmers Union advice is that 'dogs should always be under close control around livestock but if you are feeling threatened by cattle the advice is to drop the lead to allow your dog to run away'.

Safety and emergencies

Walking the Dales Way is normally a safe activity, but think ahead about how to handle an emergency, as well as taking precautions to avoid one. For short distances, the Way runs along or beside public roads: walk on the right side to face oncoming traffic, be aware of sight lines near corners and keep to the verge wherever possible. If you are walking in low light, take extra care to see and be seen, if necessary with high-visibility clothing or a torch.

The most frequent cause of danger from darkness is an over-optimistic itinerary, especially between October and March: see page 8. Consider both the hours of daylight and your likely departure time (given that you may wish first to enjoy a cooked breakfast), before deciding what daily distance you should commit to. Allow for unexpected delays.

In general, it is safer to walk with a companion than alone. That way, if anyone needs help, the uninjured walker can raise the alarm, provided that your location is known. Mobile phone coverage can be poor away from the larger towns, especially in the valleys, but you are seldom all that far from an inhabited building. If walking alone, make sure that somebody knows your intended location each evening, and if arriving late, be sure to phone to avoid causing needless concern.

In the event of serious accident or illness while on the Way, summon help by phone: dial 999 or 112 and ask for the police, then Mountain Rescue. Be ready to state your location, details of the injury/accident and your contact phone number. Most walkers carry smartphones: download the free app *OS Locate* before heading off. Its instant, accurate location finding might save your life or somebody else's. And remember that a smartphone becomes useless deadweight if you allow its battery to go flat. Unless you are good at managing your battery levels, carry a power bank or some alternative source.

During and after heavy rainfall, flooding may be a risk, and rivers can rise very rapidly. Check the weather forecast before you set off, and keep checking while on the trail. Use alternative paths or roads if need be. Do not enter flood water, and keep clear of river banks which may have become unstable when the river is in spate.

Flooded road near the A6

Accommodation and refreshments

Ilkley and Bowness offer a wide range of accommodation and facilities at both ends of the Way, but in between, choice is limited. It is important to book well in advance, especially in season and if your budget is limited. If booking for yourself, start with the most difficult or sparse locations and work towards the easier ones. Alternatively, many holiday companies offer a complete booking service, usually with baggage transfer (which is also available separately from other companies). See page 86 for details of support services.

Pubs and home-owners offering bed and breakfast (B&B) are the most widespread type of accommodation, but in the period 2020-25 many went over to self-catering or closed. Those that survived had to increase their prices markedly. Many B&Bs charge the same (or very nearly) for sole occupancy as for two people sharing. If you can find a hotel with a single room in a suitable location, that will usually be cheaper.

Note that some hotels and B&Bs impose two-night minimum stays, especially at weekends and in popular locations. This is unlikely to work for the unsupported walker, unless in the early part of the trail in Wharfedale where you can use a local bus to get back and forth. Some, such as The George, Hubberholme, charge a small premium for single-night stays – modest in relation to the extra work that such stays involve.

The table on page 15 lists all the main places with facilities that we knew to be still active in late 2025. Note that the distance offroute column refers to the distance from the *nearest* point on the Way which may not be the start or end of a section. For example, Sedbergh is only 900 m offroute from Millthrop, whereas our section ends at Lincoln's Inn Bridge which is 3·6 miles (5·8 km) further along the trail. From there, you are closer to the farm B&Bs in the Low Branthwaite area than to Sedbergh.

Red Lion Hotel, Burnsall

Table 2: Facilities along the Way

	km offroute	B&B / hotel	hostel / barn bunkhouse/glamping	campsite	pub / café	shop
Ilkley		✓	✓	✓	✓	✓
Addingham	0·5	✓		✓	✓	✓
Bolton Bridge	0·3	✓			✓	
Bolton Abbey (village)	0·4	✓			✓	
Cavendish Pavilion					✓	
Howgill	0·4		✓	✓	✓	
Appletreewick	1·0	✓		✓	✓	
Burnsall		✓			✓	
Grassington		✓	✓		✓	✓
Kettlewell		✓	✓	✓	✓	
Starbotton	0·5	✓		✓	✓	
Buckden	0·3	✓		✓	✓	✓
Hubberholme		✓			✓	
Swarthghyll			✓ ♦			
Far Gearstones		✓ ♦				
Ribblehead	2·4	✓	✓		✓	
Cowgill (Sportsmans)		✓			✓	
Dent	0·3	✓		✓	✓	✓
Sedbergh	0·9	✓	✓	✓	✓	✓
Lincoln's Inn Bridge				✓		
Low Branthwaite area ♦♦		✓				
Grayrigg (Springwood)	1·0			✓		
Kendal ♦♦♦	2·9	✓	✓	✓	✓	✓
Burneside	0·5	✓			✓	✓
Staveley	0·6	✓			✓	✓
Bowness	0·6	✓		✓	✓	✓
Windermere rail / bus station	2·7	✓	✓		✓	✓

♦ home-made evening meals/other food by arrangement
♦♦ refers to two farms, Bramaskew (at mile 58·4) and Ash Hining (0·7 miles/1·1 km offroute)
♦♦♦ Kendal is 1·8 miles (2·9 km) offroute from the Way's closest point (mile 68·5, Gilthwaiterigg Lane), or more easily reached by taxi or train from Burneside.
Nearly all campsites and some B&Bs are closed out of season: actual dates vary. Pubs, cafés and shops in rural areas often have restricted opening hours and may be closed completely on certain days (typically Mondays and Tuesdays) or for weeks/months off-season.

For budget accommodation, there is a hostel at Kettlewell, with private rooms as well as dormitory, and there are various bunk barns (e.g. Grassington), glamping sites and pods. Before booking, check whether you need to bring or hire anything (e.g. a towel or sleeping bag) and ask about your evening meal options. Cheaper still would be camping, but at the price of either carrying a heavy load or booking baggage transfer. Farmers will sometimes allow you to pitch a tent: always ask permission first.

When booking B&Bs in smaller places, ask about evening meals. Staffing shortages in rural England mean that many pubs have to close on certain weekdays, especially Mondays and Tuesdays, and some (e.g. the Sun Inn, Dent) no longer serve food at all. Your host may be willing, by prior arrangement, to drive you to and from the nearest option or even offer to make a meal. Always ask in advance, and take nothing for granted.

Accommodation clusters are found around Grassington and Sedbergh, albeit with less choice than around Ilkley and Bowness. Between Hubberholme and Cowgill, the only options we know of are Swarthghyll Farm (Walkers' Flats with food by arrangement) and Far Gearstones. The latter refers to the Shepherds Cottage, which is on the Way but has only three bedrooms. The alternative is to walk to Ribblehead (Station Inn and Bunk Barn), adding 1·5 miles (2·4 km) extra distance each way.

If you are having difficulties over accommodation, it's worth checking **airbnb.co.uk** but remember the importance of exact location, and the fact that baggage transfer services are unlikely to be able to work with this choice. If budget is the main issue, going offroute will widen your choice: for example Kendal has a wide choice including a Premier Inn, and can be reached by taxi or train from Burneside, or by walking 1·8 miles (2·9 km) from mile 68·5.

There is no food shopping on the route between Ilkley and Grassington, nor between Buckden and Dent, nor between Sedbergh and Burneside, so carry all you need for the day, and be sure to stay well-hydrated. If you don't want to carry all the water you need, you could treat water with tablets, drops or filtration.

Contactless payment is widely accepted in most shops and pubs, but even in late 2025 at least one B&B in a strategic location accepted cash only. Some shops and pubs may be willing to provide cashback with suitable purchases, but it is wise to carry plenty of sterling in case of need.

Train crossing Dent Head Viaduct

Travel planning

Ilkley is about 18 miles north-west of Leeds, but only ten miles north-west of Leeds-Bradford airport. From the airport, a direct taxi is fastest, but public transport is cheaper: take an A3 Flyer bus to Guiseley (journey time about 15 minutes) then a train to Ilkley (Northern Trains, a further 15 minutes). For contact details for public transport, see page 86.

If arriving at Leeds by train, the service to Ilkley is every half-hour (hourly on Sundays) and takes under 30 minutes. From Manchester Airport, take a train to Leeds (journey time about 90 minutes) and change there for an Ilkley train.

Between Ilkley and Buckden, the DalesBus 874 runs year-round twice daily on Sundays, with frequent stops including Addingham, Bolton Abbey, Burnsall, Grassington, Kettlewell and Starbotton. In season, usually Easter to mid-October, there is also the DalesBus 72A (schooldays only) and 72B (Saturdays and school holidays) between Grassington and Buckden. These routes provide an option to break your journey differently and ride the bus to and from an overnight base. But you need to check the timetable carefully, and be aware of when school termtime applies: see page 86 for details.

The Settle-Carlisle railway offers surely the most romantic of all public transport. Dent is the highest mainline station in England, and in under ten minutes the train reaches Ribblehead, having crossed two viaducts (Arten Gill and Dent Head) and emerged from Blea Moor's 1·5-mile tunnel. A train to Ribblehead lets you stay at the Station Inn within a stone's throw of the most magnificent of viaducts. And the service is frequent and reliable enough that you can return to Dent next morning to resume your walk. Whether you approach Dent station from above (having followed the Watershed Alternative) or from below (having climbed steeply from Lea Yeat) the trip to Ribblehead makes a memorable addition to your Dales Way.

Main road and rail routes

In the western parts of the Way, bus services are sparse but Stagecoach runs a useful 555 service between Kendal and Keswick which passes through Staveley, Windermere and Bowness. From Bowness, most people will leave via Windermere train station, less than 2 miles away, reaching it by Stagecoach bus 599 or by walking: see pages 78 and 80.

Northern Trains have frequent services daily from Windermere to Manchester and its airport (some changing at Oxenholme) with a journey time of about 2¼ hours. For Leeds, change at Preston or Manchester Piccadilly. For other destinations, it's 20 minutes to Oxenholme where you can take mainline trains northbound (for Glasgow, or Edinburgh via TransPennine Express) or southbound (for Manchester, Birmingham and London) with Avanti West Coast.

Local words and placenames

Most of the following words come from Old Norse, the language of the Vikings who arrived in the ninth century.

beck	stream	how	knoll, small hill
chase	former hunting ground	laithe	Dales barn
combe	hillside hollow	moor	heather upland
dale	valley	moss	peat bog
ewe	adult female sheep	Riding	three Ridings comprised the pre-1974 county of Yorkshire
fell	hill, moorland, mountain		
gill	ravine, mountain stream	rigg	ridge
ginnel	narrow passage between buildings in town/village	scar	cliff
		tarn	small upland lake
hogg	a young sheep, before its first shearing	tup	adult male sheep used for breeding

Packing checklist

The checklist below refers to your daytime needs, and is divided into essential and desirable. Experienced walkers may disagree about our categories, but this list makes a starting-point. Normally you will be wearing the first three or four items and carrying the rest in your rucksack.

Essential
- comfortable, waterproof walking shoes or boots
- specialist walking socks
- breathable clothing in layers
- waterproof jacket and over-trousers
- hat and gloves
- guidebook
- in case of injury, whistle and torch for attracting attention
- water carrier and plenty of water (or purification tablets/drops)
- enough food to last between supply points
- first aid kit including blister treatment
- toiletries and overnight necessities
- insect repellent and sun protection (summer)
- rucksack
- waterproof rucksack cover or liner, e.g. bin (garbage) bag
- credit/debit cards with some cash as backup.

Contactless payment is widely accepted, and there are some cash machines (ATMs) in places along the Way. Bin bags have many uses e.g. to store wet clothing or prevent hypothermia.

Ribblehead Viaduct

Desirable
- walking pole(s)
- compass, GPS device and/or smartphone (see last item)
- binoculars: useful for spotting wildlife
- camera (ideally light and rugged), also spare batteries and memory cards
- secure pockets, to keep small items handy but safe
- gaiters (defence against mud and water, also ticks)
- toilet tissue (biodegradable)
- small bags for snacks and litter
- spare socks: changing socks at lunchtime can relieve damp feet
- spare shoes (e.g. trainers, crocs or trekking sandals)
- notebook and pen
- smartphone: useful for arrangements but don't rely on one for emergencies; reception can be patchy
- if you depend on your phone, take a power bank or spare battery.

Camping
If you are camping, you need much more kit, including tent, sleeping gear, camping stove, fuel, cooking utensils and food. Your rucksack will need to be larger e.g. 45-85 litres, and could be 5-15 kg heavier. Previous experience is advisable.

2·1 Geology and scenery

During the Ice Ages, glaciers deepened and straightened the main valleys and smeared the hills with boulder clay. Melt-water flooded the valleys and left behind silt, sand and gravel. We describe below the solid rocks you'll see on the Way from south to north.

Ilkley to Appletreewick: millstones

Ilkley's famous Moor and many of its buildings are made of millstone grit, a coarse-grained sandstone. It is exposed at the Strid (see page 40) and forms the bedrock as far as the Craven Fault near Appletreewick.

Appletreewick to Dent: limestones

Limestone pavement has developed between Grassington and Kettlewell. Joints have been widened by naturally acidic rain that dissolves the rock. The Carboniferous limestone blocks are known as clints, and the vertical gaps in between as grikes.

The Wharfe valley between Kettlewell and Buckden has a glaciated U-shape. The flat floor was once the bed of a lake dammed by glacial debris. The valley sides are formed of alternating bands of limestone, sandstone and shale called the Yoredale Series.

Beyond Hubberholme, limestone appears in the river bed. In drier times the water flows underground in passages. West of Cam Houses there are shake holes – conical depressions where the clay has slumped into solution holes in the limestone.

> **Yorkshire Dales National Park**
> The Yorkshire Dales National Park was designated in 1954 and is the living, working home of about 24,000 people, including over 1000 farms. The YDNP authority has to balance their needs with those of visitors: in 2023 the Park had a total of 6.7 million visitor days, contributing nearly £500 million to the local economy. The Way passes the NP Centre at Grassington (tel 01756 751 690): see page 44 bullet 3.
>
> The Dales Way runs within the YDNP for 56 miles/90 km from Bolton Bridge to Crook of Lune. The visible geology make it a classic area for education as well as recreation. People have cleared woodland, improved lowland pastures, and built stone walls, barns and villages to create the much-loved Dales landscape. Until the 1870s they also mined lead, but nowadays tourism and sheep farming are the main economic activities: www.yorkshiredales.org.uk.

The Three Peaks (see page 54) are capped by millstone grit above the Yoredale Series on a platform of carboniferous limestone. The whaleback mounds near Ribblehead are drumlins, composed of material transported by ice sheets and left behind as they melted.

As you approach Dent, the corrie at Combe Scar comes into view, and the hills beyond take on a subtly different appearance. This marks the line of the Dent Fault.

Dent to Bowness: the oldest rocks

The Dent Fault runs from the north, crossing the dale near Barth Bridge and continuing up Barbondale. The bedrocks ahead are Silurian mudstones, sandstones and silts more than 400 million years old.

The Howgill Fells are composed of hard and uniform sandstone. The contorted pale grey strata in the channels of the Rawthey and Lune bear witness to the unimaginable forces at work in the Earth's crust.

Turning west at Lowgill, you see the distant jagged profiles of the Lake District. The highest ridges are composed of rocks called the Borrowdale Volcanics, which erupted some 450 million years ago. Later they were uplifted into mountains of Himalayan height, located north of the warm sea where carboniferous limestone was forming. The erosion of that range formed the millstone grit of Ilkley Moor.

Adam Sedgwick

As a young man, Adam Sedgwick (1785-1873) studied the differences in the landscape and the changes in strata exposed in the river beds in and around Dentdale. Born at Dent vicarage, he went to Sedbergh School and studied maths and theology at Trinity College, Cambridge. From 1818 until his death, he was Woodwardian Professor of Geology at Cambridge.

Sedgwick's eminence coincided with the rise of geology as a young science. Like many notable scientists, he struggled to reconcile his deeply-held religious beliefs with emerging scientific theories, and he condemned Darwin's book on the origin of species. His attachment to Dentdale was lifelong: he wrote of its history and traditions and was a generous benefactor. A granite fountain in Dent commemorates his life: see photograph below.

Sedgwick memorial, Dent

Limestone pavement at sunset

2·2 Mining, quarrying and railways

Mining

Grassington grew large amongst Dales settlements because of the lead mines on the moors to its north-east. Buckden, Dent and Starbotton had lead mines of lesser importance. Lead was probably mined near Grassington in Roman times, and the monks of Fountains Abbey (19 miles away) mined the area in the 14th century.

The peak in lead mining occurred in the late 18th and early 19th centuries. The Duke of Devonshire invested in drainage systems, new shafts, winding engines, roads and processing mills. The most productive period was after 1820, but by 1860 reserves were nearing exhaustion and imports had become cheaper. The miners began moving away, and production ended in 1880.

The waste dumps were exploited for barytes and fluorspar in the 20th century, and the remains of the industry that built Grassington can be seen on the exposed moor. For more, visit the 'Lead mining in Wharfedale' section of the YDNP website *www.yorkshiredales.org.uk* and visit Grassington Folk Museum: see the panel on page 45.

Quarrying

Overseas visitors are surprised to find people living in National Parks and astonished to see quarrying of limestone. What they are looking at, however, is a typical British compromise. The permissions to quarry were almost all issued before the Parks were created, and the cost of revoking them would be high. The mineral is in demand for roadstone, hydrated lime and concrete aggregate; and employment in the Parks prevents villages from declining into mere clusters of holiday homes.

Quarrying damages the landscape, and some early examples paid no attention to sympathetic working or appropriate restoration. Modern approaches try harder, and National Park authorities engage in dialogue with operators to improve practice.

Quarrying demands transport, but most rural roads are unsuitable for large trucks. Where rail transport is possible, it is preferable. At Swinden Quarry, west of Grassington, a recent extension of permission for deeper extraction was linked to the continuing use of rail transport. With it comes a possibility of restoring the passenger service from Skipton, and a new station near Grassington.

Swinden Quarry (aerial view)

Railways

Railways dramatically increased the accessibility of Ilkley and Windermere in the 19th century, and lines were opened to Bolton Abbey and Sedbergh. The prosperity of the middle classes promoted the idea of holidays at the same time as poets and artists were arousing interest in scenic beauty. It was not until 1902 that the Yorkshire Dales Railway completed its Grassington Branch, by which time Grassington's population had declined to its lowest ebb. The town grew again as a holiday destination and as a dormitory for Bradford, with houses built near the station.

The Settle-Carlisle line, near the midpoint of the Dales Way is arguably the most scenic railway in England. Its 72 miles of track includes 14 tunnels and 21 viaducts, including the iconic Ribblehead Viaduct with its 24 arches. Work began in 1869 and took seven years. Some 6000 men built the line, many living in temporary 'towns' amongst the bleak fells. Smallpox caused many deaths, and memorials along the line commemorate some of the men who died in accidents.

British Railways proposed closing the line in the 1960s and again in the early 1980s. The latter proposal was based on low passenger numbers and the high cost of repairing the viaduct at Ribblehead, now the symbol of the line. Opposition was intense at local and national level. The line was reprieved, and a marketing plan was launched to attract more passengers. Stations that had been closed were refurbished and reopened, and Ribblehead now also serves as a Visitor Information Centre.

The regular passenger service today comprises diesel trains with occasional steam and diesel charter trains. The line is a tourist attraction in its own right, as well as a wonderful resource for walkers, including those on the Dales Way. For information on the line, including guided walks, visit *settle-carlisle.co.uk*.

Leander hauling the Fellsman up the 'Long Drag' to Ribblehead

2·3 Farming, tourism and conservation

Farming

Farming maintains the scenery that draws many tourists to the Dales and Lakes, and conservation is often the arbiter between them.

Late in the 18th century, farming changed radically. The industrial towns were expanding, and demand for food increased. Many of the characteristic stone walls were built at that time, to manage animals and fodder crops. Field barns were constructed to house cattle in winter and to store hay.

You will see many old lime kilns along the Way (between Grassington and Kettlewell, near Yockenthwaite and in Dentdale): see page 46. Burning limestone (calcium carbonate) mixed with coal creates quicklime (calcium oxide) which helps to fertilise and condition farmland.

The isolation of the Dales communities was reduced when better roads and railways were built. Subsistence crops grown in more favoured districts were brought in, allowing grass to become the most important Dales crop, and animals and dairy produce were sent more readily to market.

Hill farming is a hard job with little financial reward. Traditional methods are in decline, replaced by modern materials, mechanisation and chemical fertiliser. Modern methods may threaten the very things that make the National Parks special.

Hill farming year

April	Lambing time. Hoggs [older lambs] return from winter pasture.
May	Ewes and hoggs are moved to higher pasture. Cattle begin calving and are turned out to grazing. Meadows are muck spread or fertilised.
June	Silage is cut and baled for winter feed. Hoggs are sheared.
July	Ewes are sheared and dipped to kill parasites. Wild flower meadows are at their best. Hay time.
August	Second silage cut is taken where possible. Walling repairs begin. Lambs separated from ewes and bulls put with cows. Traditional agricultural shows take place.
September & October	Ewes are dipped for sale at autumn markets. Breeding and fatstock lambs and suckler calves are sold. Autumn calving takes place. Walling continues.
November	Tupping [breeding] time. Hoggs are sent away for winter. Cattle are housed for the winter. Winter muck spreading.
December	Indoor maintenance and repairs. Cattle vaccinations (pneumonia).
January & February	Sheep are brought down to lower fields during snow. Sheep are scanned and those with twins are kept housed.
March	Increase in care needed for spring calving cattle and ewes in lamb. Preparation for lambing. Fertiliser dressing for meadows.

This summary is based on information from the YDNP website www.yorkshiredales.org.uk which also hosts four videos on farming through the seasons.

Tourism

Tourism began when artists and writers started visiting the countryside in the 18th century. Railways made tourism possible for the masses by the late 19th century, but the boom came with car ownership in the second half of the 20th century.

The huge influx of visitors can cause conflict with those trying to work. Crop damage and interference with farming activities are common complaints. It is inevitable that the very presence of large numbers of people detracts from the peaceful beauty that many of them wish to experience.

Tourism brings much-needed income to village businesses such as shops, pubs, tea rooms and B&Bs. Some farms have diversified into the hospitality sector, offering B&B and camping barns, and converting redundant buildings into self-catering properties.

Lake District National Park

You enter the LDNP beyond Burneside (see page 75), and the Park extends far beyond Bowness. Created in 1951, it's not only England's largest National Park, it also became a UNESCO World Heritage Site in 2017. The Park includes England's largest lake (Windermere), deepest lake (Wastwater), highest point (Scafell Pike) and wettest place (Seatoller). Sheep farming maintains its landscape in a form loved by generations of hill-walkers.

In 2022, over 18 million people visited the Lake District, with an average stay of 3.6 nights. Such large numbers pose various threats to the landscape, especially where focused on a handful of honeypot destinations in summer months. In addition to erosion from excessive footfall, rising demand for water has led to engineering works by water suppliers on lakes such as Thirlmere and Haweswater. For more, visit **lakedistrict.gov.uk**.

Conservation

Two National Parks, the Yorkshire Dales and Lake District, are home to 80% of the Way's length: see the panels above and on page 20. The NP Authorities have a duty to conserve and enhance natural beauty, wildlife and cultural heritage, and to promote opportunities for the public to understand and enjoy the special qualities of the area. While doing so, they also seek to foster its economic and social wellbeing.

Conserving the variety of living species in various habitats is challenge enough. It's a difficult balancing act to protect some of the Parks' other attributes at the same time. Conflict inevitably surfaces when conservation – of archaeological features, buildings, barns, walls, farming traditions and limestone pavements – is in tension with efficient quarrying or farming, or with the growing demands of recreation.

Managing open access and providing for visitors is part of the purpose of the National Parks. Looking after the Dales Way is just one of many demands on their resources.

Feeding sheep in winter

2·4 Habitats and wildlife

There are five main habitats along the Way:
- upland moor
- hay meadow
- blanket bog/acid grassland
- limestone pavement/grassland
- rivers and lakes

Upland moor

Upland moor is found on higher ground, for example the millstone grit of Ilkley Moor and the hilltops between Bolton Abbey and Burnsall. Its thin acidic soil mainly supports heather with some bilberry. Heather carpets the moorland in purple flowers in late July and August. This habitat is vulnerable to encroaching bracken, especially in areas of over-grazing. On Ilkley Moor, progress has been made in combating bracken and restoring traditional vegetation.

Heather provides shelter and food for the red grouse, a game bird in season from 12 August to 10 December. Identify red grouse by its abrupt take-off, low flight and loud call 'ge-back, ge-back, ge-back-back-back'. Bird life is sparse, but you are sure to see meadow pipits, small birds with olive-brown upper parts and a paler underside.

Meadow pipit

Hay meadow

Hay meadows are present on the valley floors and lower slopes. They provide crucial food to insects and birds and are an intrinsic part of the Dales field-and-barn landscape. Nationally, it is reported that more than 90% of traditionally managed hay meadows have been lost since 1945 – a huge loss of havens for wild flowers. They are a major feature of summer walking in the Dales.

Farm animals are moved to higher ground in May (see page 24) and grasses and flowers allowed to flourish. The cranesbill meadows are the least 'agriculturally improved' land in this National Park, and their biodiversity is recognised internationally. Wood cranesbill is a key indicator of species-rich hay meadow. Like meadow cranesbill, it grows wild in meadows and on roadside verges.

Heather moorland; red grouse (inset)

Wild flowers support many insects, including butterflies, dragonflies and damselflies. Wharfedale has a range of native species and hosts many summer migrant butterflies, including the peacock, painted lady and red admiral.

Blanket bog and acid grassland

Blanket bog and acid grassland are found on high ground. Blanket bog occurs on the Yoredale Series and millstone grit, usually on deep peat which is waterlogged. Sphagnum moss and cotton grass are the dominant plants. Wet acid grassland develops on poorly drained soils at high elevation, and sometimes lower down after over-grazing. It is home to a limited variety of plants and is of low grazing value.

Peacock butterfly

Curlew

The curlew, Britain's largest wader, breeds in damp open country. Distinguished by its upward-burbling call (sounds like an old-fashioned whistling kettle), it has long legs and a long, downward-curved bill.

The lapwing is a medium-sized black and white bird with rounded wings and a distinctive crest. It breeds here and on moorland, where its distinctive 'pee-wit' call is heard. The golden plover is similar in size, but more likely to be heard than seen when it broadcasts its mournful, single-note call from a distant hummock.

Wood cranesbill with meadow buttercup; golden plover (inset)

Limestone pavement/grassland

Limestone pavement provides a unique habitat, see pages 20-21: in its grikes, rare plants are sheltered from grazing animals. The thin soils produce a rich sward of lime-loving plants.

In addition to curlew, lapwing and meadow pipit, you may see buzzard circling high above. A large bird of prey, its wingspan is about one metre (3 ft 3 in) – only half that of an eagle. Its wings are broad and rounded, with pale underwing markings. In flight it often soars, holding its wings in a shallow V-shape.

Wild thyme

Above the hay meadows, stone walls enclose limestone grassland where round-horned Swaledale sheep graze. Stoats are agile hunters, and you may spot one scurrying to hide among the stones. (Weasel are smaller, with a shorter tail that lacks the stoat's distinctive black tip.)

Stoat

Rivers and lakes

Rivers and lakes provide various important habitats, and river valleys act as wildlife corridors. River bank erosion and increased use of drainage and chemicals pose threats. Fly-fishing for trout is important on the larger rivers.

Swaledale sheep (ram)

Many species of bird flourish near and on the water. Wagtails are common, especially pied (black-and-white) and grey (with yellow underparts, see below). Much rarer is the yellow wagtail, a summer migrant. Mallards, goosanders and red-breasted mergansers are common on the River Wharfe.

You may be lucky enough to see the brilliant blue-green flash of a kingfisher in flight. The dipper is more common – a small, dark-brown bird with white breast, often seen perched on a rock in a fast-flowing stream. It walks underwater in search of insect larvae, using the pressure of the current to give it traction on the stream bed.

Kingfisher

Lake Windermere formed after glaciers gouged a valley which filled with melt-water. It is 60 metres deep in parts, and it provides a variety of habitats including shallow bays, reed beds, wooded shorelines and lakeshore wetlands. Recreational and agricultural effluent can easily damage these habitats, reducing them to a pebble beach with hardly any plant or animal life. The lake is important for resident and over-wintering birds, a wide range of aquatic plants and several species of fish – including the arctic charr, a salmonid fish originally from the seas around Iceland.

Grey wagtail

Red-breasted merganser

2·5 The religious heritage

Our front cover shows the ruins of Bolton Priory. Founded in the 12th century, much of it was wrecked during the Dissolution of the Monasteries in 1539. Its last prior, Richard Moone, managed to save the nave of the priory church, which remains an active parish church to this day. Building of the great west tower began in 1520, but was halted in 1539 and never finished.

The Victorian restoration took place during 1853-80, mainly directed by George Street, with notable stained glass windows by Augustus Pugin. By the late 1970s serious disrepair had set in. Canon Maurice Slaughter led a campaign to fund refurbishment in 1982-85, when the west tower was glazed, floored and roofed.

Entering the church by its impressive west porch, you pass through the west tower to the nave. Its east wall separates the restored church from the ruined choir. It was painted in 1880 by local craftsmen (Thomas Bottomley assisted by R H Greenwood). The five Madonna lilies represent the Priory's dedication to St Mary. The lilies alternate with six other plants (barley, olive, vine, passion flower, rose and palm) symbolising various events and sayings in the life of Jesus.

Bolton Priory interior

Most of the English monasteries were established shortly after the Norman Conquest of England in 1066. Many of the monks came from Europe to face the challenge of living a simple life in a fierce, wild land.

The monks practised sheep farming around their monasteries, later developing outlying farms as 'granges'. Coverham Abbey established a grange near Dent and initiated schooling in the valley. The monasteries grew rich on the wool trade, and the life of the monks became easier. The perception grew that moral standards were declining in some religious orders and some clerics were meddling in politics.

Henry VIII broke away from the Church of Rome when he was unable to obtain a divorce from his first wife, Catherine of Aragon. He declared himself head of the Church in England in 1534. To help finance his extravagant spending, he seized the buildings and possessions of the smaller monasteries. Monks were dispersed to other monasteries, lead was stripped from their roofs, and the decline began.

Bolton Priory west porch

The monasteries had provided food, shelter and often a basic education to lay employees and the faithful. Their closure was a loss to many ordinary people. A protest known as the Pilgrimage of Grace began in Yorkshire but was rapidly put down. In 1539 the king dissolved the larger monasteries, and many of the monks were forced to leave the country and continue their devotions elsewhere in Europe.

Records suggest that in 1120 there was a community of Augustinian canons at Embsay, near Skipton. In 1150 Lady Alice de Romille of Skipton Castle gave land at Bolton to the black-robed canons to establish their priory. An alternative, more romantic legend claims that Lady Alice donated the land after the death of her son, the Boy of Egremond, a nephew of the King of Scotland, who drowned at the Strid while hunting. This version is unlikely because the Boy's name appears next to his mother's in the priory's charter. Whatever the truth, romance lives on in Wordsworth's epic poems and the paintings of Landseer, Ruskin and Turner.

Although the building is commonly known as Bolton Abbey, strictly the ruins are of the Priory Church of St Mary and St Cuthbert: see the panel on page 40 for visitor information.

Bolton Priory exterior

Quakerism, George Fox and Margaret Fell

In the mid-17th century, England was a centre of radical religious thought, with many dissident Protestant groups opposed to the Catholic idea that people can communicate with God only through a priest. In 1652, a radical new preacher managed to unite many of these groups into a single movement. George Fox (1624-1691) questioned the need for organised church structures and he became the father of Quakerism.

Following his vision on Pendle Hill, Fox gained huge support when he preached outside St Andrews Church Sedbergh: see page 64. On 13 June 1652, he spoke fluently and passionately for three or more hours to an outdoor audience of over 1000 on nearby Firbank Fell. His critique was of the 'false church' with its hireling priests, 'steeplehouses' (his dismissive word for churches) and tithes. He argued that instead of listening to priests, people should discover the divinely inspired 'light within' themselves. He viewed men and women as equal before God.

After his Sermon on the Fell, Fox travelled to Swarthmoor Hall, Ulverston, where he stayed with Thomas and Margaret Fell. He immediately persuaded Margaret of his radical views, and for 50 years until her death she became a Quaker leader and organiser. Whilst George Fox was the father of Quakerism, Margaret Fell was truly its mother. Quakers were in danger at a time when people were imprisoned for their religious beliefs. Official toleration did not arrive until the Act of 1689 by which time Fox's health had been broken by appalling conditions in his years of imprisonment. He barely survived until 1691.

Two of our guidebooks cover the Fox/Fell story: *Friends Way 1 and 2* are devoted to George Fox's and Margaret Fell's journeys, marriage and imprisonments: for details, see page 87. *Friends Way 2* ends at Swarthmoor Hall which became the first headquarters of the movement. It hosted regular Meetings – including, from 1671, monthly Women's Meetings, of which Margaret and her daughters were prominent leaders.

For Dales Way walkers, it's easy to visit two Meetinghouses whose simple interiors have barely changed in 350 years, their layouts evoking the democratic atmosphere of Meetings. The Way passes Farfield, which stands open during daylight hours: see page 38. With a small detour, you can take in Brigflatts (1675) near Sedbergh: see page 65. For a deeper understanding, spend an extra day in Sedbergh to complete the 9·4-mile Quaker Trail circuit (mapped in both *Friends Way* books).

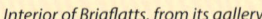

Interior of Brigflatts, from its gallery

3.1 Link Routes to Ilkley

The concept of a footpath from the industrial cities to the Lake District inspired the Ramblers Association to promote Link Routes from Bradford and Leeds to the start of the Dales Way at Ilkley. A route from Harrogate followed later, originally joining the Way near Bolton Priory, but the current route (published in 2010) joins at Ilkley.

The Link Routes are shown at small scale below. All three are waymarked to some extent, but you are advised to carry and refer to our map booklet that shows them in detail at 1:40,000, courtesy of the LDWA: see page 87. For a text description of the routes, refer to Colin Speakman's excellent book in which they occupy pages 92-110: see page 87.

The Bradford Link is 12·5 mi (20 km) and starts from near Bradford Cathedral. After 3·7 miles (6 km) it passes Shipley station and Saltaire, soon leaving the urban area to cross Bingley, Burley and Ilkley Moors, with a high point near the Twelve Apostles stone circle. The Leeds and Harrogate Links are both longer and would extend your Dales Way expedition by one or two full days.

At 20·5 miles (33 km), the Leeds Link at would be daunting to many walkers as a single day, but using public transport lets you split it into convenient sections. It starts very close to the Town Hall of the UK's third most populous city, but quickly becomes quite rural in character.

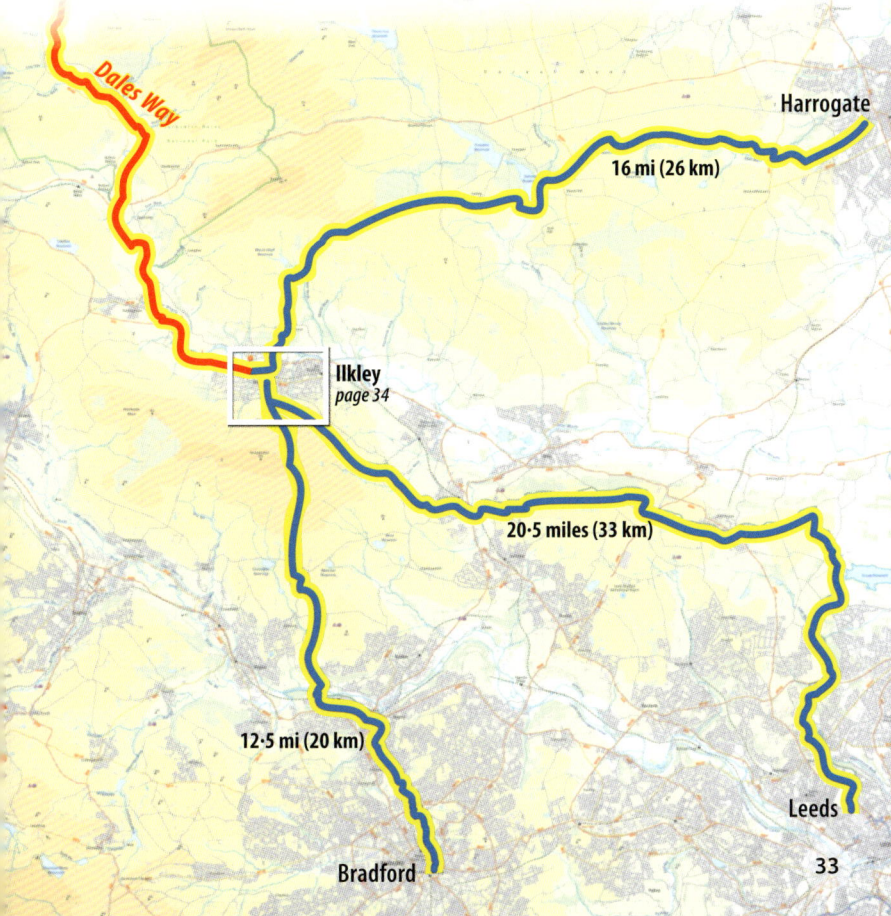

The route runs close to streams for several miles, traversing public parks and woods. It crosses farmland near the village of Eccup to join with the Ebor Way. It continues through fields and woods to cross heather moorland on Otley Chevin, high above Wharfedale. It ends along the edge of Ilkley Moor, passing the Cow and Calf Rocks on its descent to Ilkley.

The Harrogate Link is 16 miles (26 km) long, and a shortage of accommodation and public transport makes it difficult to split. It begins in the town centre at the Pump Room and heads west through the Valley Gardens. It crosses woods and rolling pastures to the Washburn valley reservoirs, then heather moorland, ending with panoramic views of Wharfedale and Ilkley Moor.

Cow and Calf Rocks

Ilkley

Ilkley was a small village which expanded into a thriving spa town in Victorian times. Nowadays, the main shopping and civic areas based on The Grove, Station Road and Brook Street hint at the fashionable glory of those days. About 15,200 people live here (2024 data), and the town centre is pleasingly compact. Opposite the train and bus station you'll find the helpful Visitor Information Centre, open Mon-Sat 09.30-16.30 except 12.30-13.00 (shorter hours out of season): tel 01943 436 232.

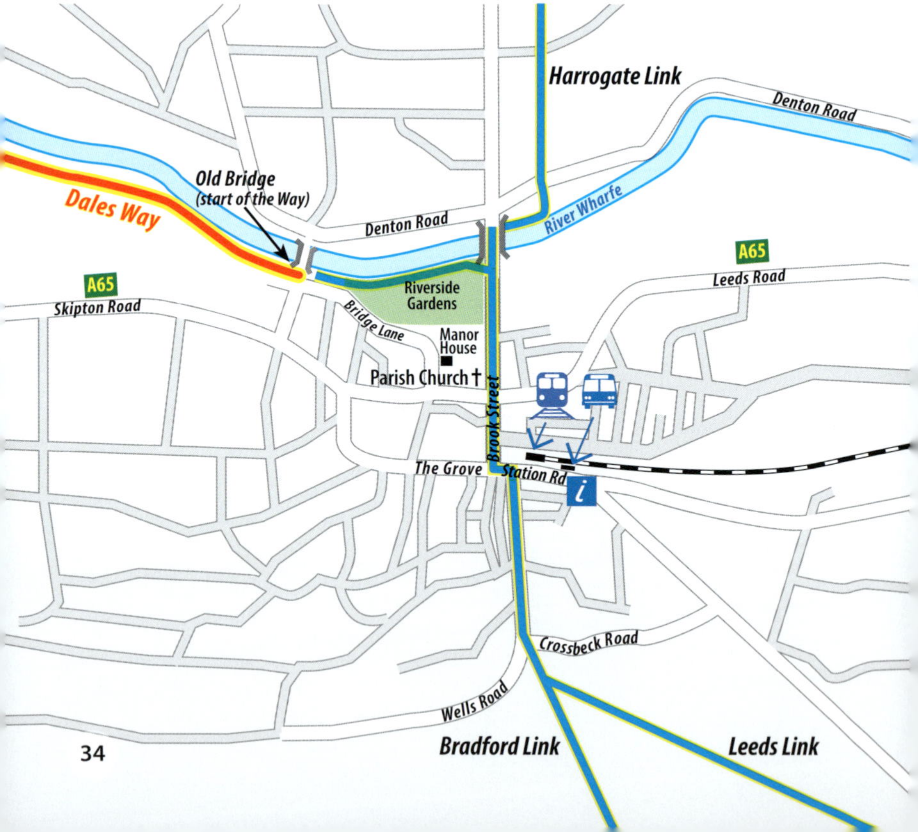

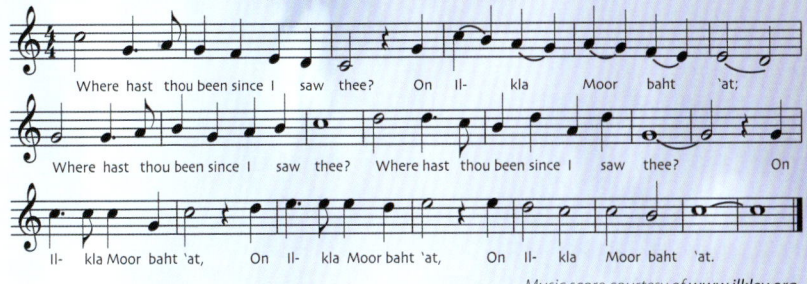

Music score courtesy of www.ilkley.org

Ilkley today is a centre for tourism and shopping, as well as a base for commuters to Leeds and Bradford. Located on the northern edge of Ilkley Moor, it was one of the first 'Walkers are Welcome' towns. Ilkley Moor became world-famous long ago through the Yorkshire anthem 'On Ilkla Moor Baht 'At'.

Signs of early settlement are found around All Saints' Parish Church, which was built on the site of Olicana, a Roman fort; in 1925, two Roman altars were discovered built into its 15th century tower. The oldest part of the present building is its 13th century south doorway, but the church has been extended and restored, notably in 1860-61 and 1927. Three superb 8th century Saxon crosses in its graveyard were rescued from erosion damage, restored and now stand on display inside.

The nearby Manor House is a historic Listed Building dating from c. 1390 and houses a museum and art gallery. Flint tools found on Ilkley Moor show that mesolithic people visited the area, whilst cup-and-ring carvings and the Swastika Stone bear witness to settlement by neolithic farmers. It is open every weekend, normally 11.00 to 16.00, admission free.

Saxon Crosses, All Saints' Parish Church

Heather on Ilkley Moor

3·2 Ilkley to Burnsall

Distance 13·2 miles 21·2 km
Terrain well-defined field paths, surfaced paths, roads (less than 10%)
Grade gently rising path with no significant climbs or descents
Food and drink Addingham, Bolton Abbey, Cavendish Pavilion, Howgill, Appletreewick (1 km offroute), Burnsall
Summary easy walking beside the River Wharfe; religious points of interest include St Peter's and Farfield (Quaker), and scenic highlights include Bolton Priory and the Strid

mile 0	2·6		3·6		3·2		3·8	13·2
Ilkley		4·2 St Peters		5·8 Bolton Priory		5·1 Barden Bridge	6·1	Burnsall

- From the train station (next to the bus station), turn right past La Stazione coffee shop and after 50 m go right again down Brook Street: see the town plan on page 34.
- Continue towards the River Wharfe and turn left before the road bridge down steps to the riverside path. Cross Riverside Park and pass in front of the Riverside Hotel (with public toilets just beyond). Reach Ilkley's Old Bridge, built in 1675 and still standing, albeit closed to vehicles.
- The Dales Way begins at a stone bench outside Old Bridge Nurseries, and ends at a matching bench just above Bowness: see page 78. The green fingerpost opposite announces Bowness as 82 miles away (but see page 7 about distances).

- After 250 m beside the river, continue along the tennis club access road. Just 1 km before the buildings, go left through the first of many metal kissing-gates.
- Follow Dales Way and Millennium Way Circular signs through fields and along the tranquil riverbank as far as mile 1·3 where you join the old A65 road.

Riverside Park, Ilkley

The Old Bridge, Ilkley

- Follow the road for 500 m, then turn right into Old Lane, a cul-de-sac. It leads into Low Mill, a former industrial village now turned into attractive housing. An information board explains its history.
- Keep ahead between the houses and leave by a paved ramp onto a lane. Turn right down steps to a shady path that leads towards Addingham.
- St Peter's Church appears ahead on the right. Turn left before it to reach the entrance near its bell tower and visit it if possible. It stands open during hours of daylight: see the panel.
- Afterwards, leave by the arched gateway beyond the bell tower and go ahead over a narrow stone footbridge over the Town Beck. Turn right along the road (North Street) for 100 m until it bends left. Look back for fine views of Addingham's suspension bridge.
- Leave the road at mile 2·7 to bear right down cobbled steps to the riverside. Cross a small field: a blue plaque explains it was donated by Crossley and Dawson to the Overseers of the Poor of Addingham in 1685-6.
- Pass between houses into a static caravan site. Make a right-left dogleg to exit onto open river bank.
- Continue along the river bank to mile 4·3 where the Way climbs and swings right into a wood to pass a house on your left. Cross the Bolton Road with care.

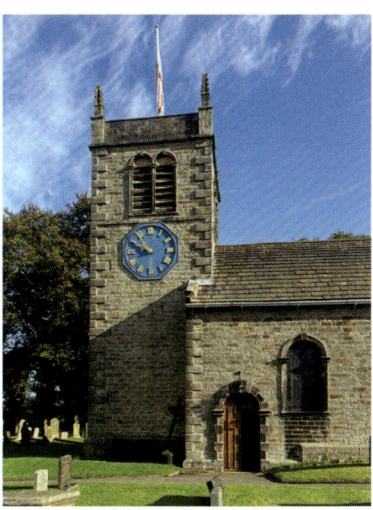
St Peter's Church, Addingham

ⓘ Addingham and St Peter's
Addingham village was a centre for weaving cotton and wool, and weaving lofts survive in some of its 18th century houses. The village's first water-powered mill dates from 1789 and produced worsted wool – high-quality yarn that is stronger and smoother than other woollens, as in tailored suits versus knitted sweaters.
St Peter's Church dates from the 12th century and houses a 9th century carved Saxon cross. The oak furniture was carved by Robert Thompson of Kilburn, with 14 examples of his trademark mouse. The tower's six bells still ring for services, and the blue-faced clock dates from the 1830s. Download a leaflet from its superb website: **stpetersaddingham.org.uk**.

Farfield Meetinghouse

- A notice at the back of Farfield, built in 1689, explains its role as one of the world's earliest Meetinghouses, sensitively restored to its Quaker simplicity. Historic England selected it in 2018 as among the top ten places in its Faith and Belief category.

- Afterwards, turn right to follow the farm road briefly, and immediately go right again over a stone wall by step-stile.

- Follow the corner of the wall on your right on a tarmac drive and continue over a gated step-stile into the next field. Cross a stone wall, and before the end of the next field, exit through a gate onto the road.

- ⚠ Cross the busy B6160 with great care, and face oncoming traffic to walk briefly on its narrow verge. Within 80 m turn right on a recent pathway that runs beside the road, partly screened from it.

- Follow it through a gate into woodland, soon turning right and crossing a small stream to follow the river bank from mile 4·9.

Gated step-stile into the field

- About 100 m later, pass under the A59 by a modern road bridge and pass Ferry House on your right to reach Bolton Bridge.

- Cross the road and go through the metal gate onto the broad grassy footpath to Bolton Priory, beside the River Wharfe. There's a handy small bench off to the right, placed in memory of the Woods of Ferry House (1994).

- You are now in the Yorkshire Dales National Park: see the panel on page 20. From here to Barden Bridge the Way crosses land owned by the Chatsworth Settlement Trustees, who allow public access.

- Follow the riverside path around a broad curve in the grassy pasture for nearly a mile to the graceful ruins of Bolton Priory at mile 6·1. Divert left to explore the ruins and see the panel on page 40 for visit information.

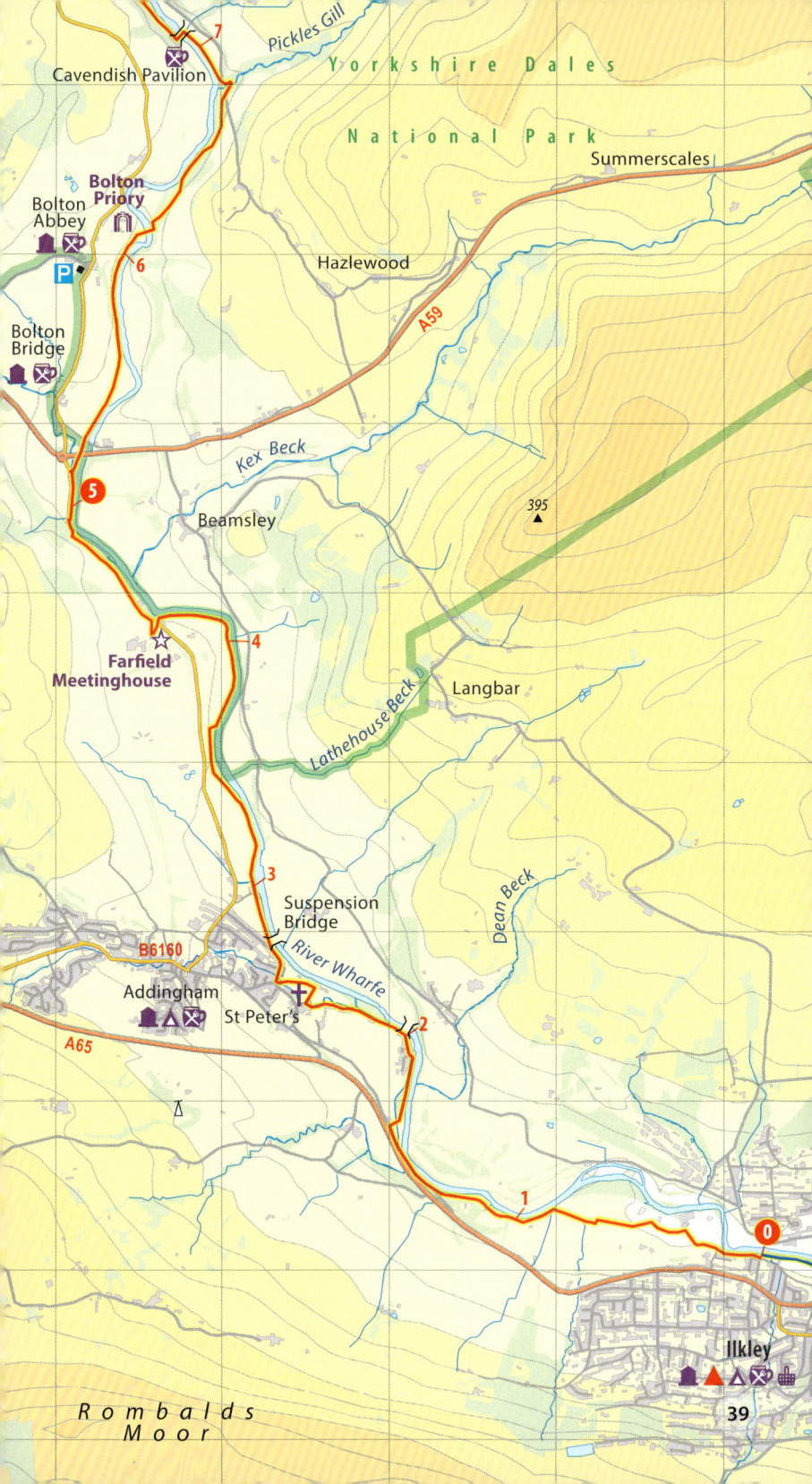

Stepping stones in front of Bolton Priory

- From the Priory, the Way crosses the river by footbridge but, if the river level permits it safely, you may prefer the stepping stones known as Friars' Steps.
- Afterwards, turn left very briefly, then bear right up steps and follow a woodland path. Look behind you for superb views back over the priory.
- The undulating path eventually descends to a ford and bridge across Pickles Gill at mile 6·8. After the bridge, resume the river bank by bearing off to the left.
- After 400 m, cross the river by the wooden footbridge to turn right into Strid Woods. Pass (or visit) the Cavendish Pavilion café (open daily from 10.00, with variable closing times).
- Stay on the broad roadway of crushed stone to mile 8·4 to reach the Strid, a historic feature: see the panel opposite. Descend across the rocks for a good view of the 2-metre gap in the gorge through which the Wharfe plunges thunderously – an awesome sight when in spate.
- Afterwards, ascend to resume the Way, continuing upstream on a narrow rocky path. The Way, soon on a broader path, climbs to a stone wall, descends again, and then forks right (unsigned) towards Barden Bridge before leaving Strid Woods.
- At mile 8·9, reach and climb steps on the left to cross the crenellated Barden Aqueduct.

> **Bolton Abbey and Bolton Priory**
> 'Bolton Abbey' refers both to the tiny village beside the B6160 and to the large surrounding estate, marketed as a visitor attraction by the Chatsworth Settlement Trustees. To visit the village, turn left on a path through a gap in the high stone wall well before the priory.
> To explore the ruins of Bolton Priory, divert left just before the stepping stones. Enter the site by either of the wooden gates at its south-east corner. Admission is free, but donations are welcome: open daily in season with shorter hours in winter (tel 01756 710 238). Visit **www.boltonpriory.org.uk** and **boltonabbey.com** and see also page 30.

River Wharfe plunging through the Strid

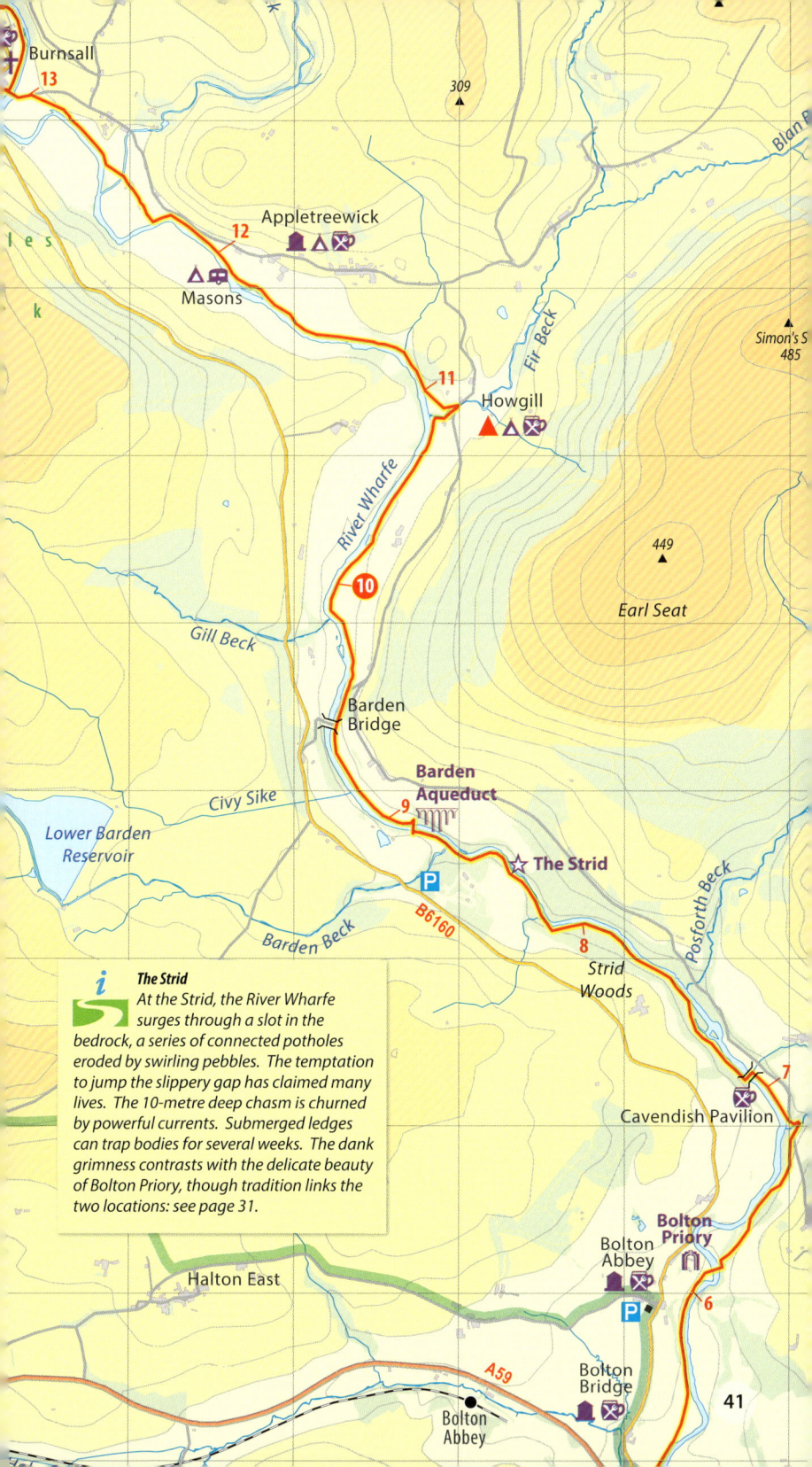

- Resume the east bank of the River Wharfe, and as you approach Barden Bridge, look left beyond the trees to glimpse Barden Tower: see the panel.
- From Barden Bridge continue upstream past the parking lay-by, and follow a narrow riverside path, at first between road and river. At mile 10·8 go through a gate into a livestock field.
- Approaching Howgill, the Way bends right past some wooden cabins and caravans to pass through farm buildings and onto a road bridge over Fir Beck.
- Immediately, turn sharp left into a short lane, cross a field and descend to the riverside, continuing upstream through a wood and into pastures where the Way descends to the riverside path.

> **Barden Tower and the Cliffords**
> Barden Tower was a derelict forest lodge until becoming home to Henry Clifford, "the Shepherd Lord". Henry, aged seven, went into hiding after his father's death in The Wars of the Roses in 1461. He lived as a shepherd before claiming his inheritance in 1485 after the defeat of the last Yorkist king. Preferring country to court, Henry turned the Tower into a fortified house where he studied astronomy and alchemy.
>
> Lady Anne Clifford had to wait 38 years for her inheritance. This redoubtable woman then restored the derelict Tower in 1657-9. She rebuilt many churches and established almshouses on her estates, which stretched north to Penrith. She also restored the castles of Skipton, Pendragon, Brough, Appleby and Brougham. For a tribute walk, see www.ladyannesway.co.uk.

- At mile 11·5 another path leads to the historic village of Appletreewick (pronounced app-trick) which is mentioned in the Domesday Book. About 800 m further on, pass Masons Campsite which (in season) offers coffee, cake and ice cream to walkers.
- Ahead looms the dark crown of Burnsall Fell, whilst the hills to your right show outcrops of limestone and traces of abandoned cultivation strips. You are crossing the Craven Fault, one of the most important geological features in England: see page 20.
- Continue along the river bank for 700 m, where the Way veers right toward a barn on a rough vehicle track. Pass between farm buildings and emerge through a gate.
- At a second gate, perhaps standing open, the track forks. At mile 12·5 bear left across Barben Beck by footbridge on the footpath to Burnsall. This rejoins the Wharfe, then climbs away from it across pasture to meet the road.
- Turn left across the river to enter the village, which has a fine parish church (St Wilfrid Burnsall) about 400 m beyond Burnsall Bridge. If you visit it, you can resume the Way by continuing up the road just beyond it to a path beside the village hall that descends to the riverside.
  - Otherwise, to continue the Way from the bridge, turn sharp right before the Red Lion Hotel, then left along the riverside path.

River Wharfe at mile 12·4

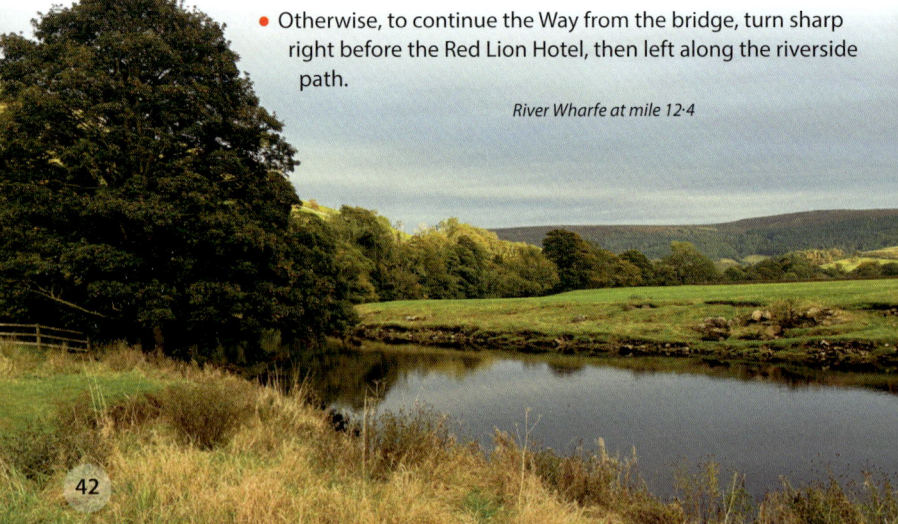

3.3 Burnsall to Buckden | 45 | 47 |

Distance 13·8 miles 22·2 km
Terrain well-defined field paths, farm tracks, roads (less than 10%)
Grade steady 200 m climb through Grassington onto limestone upland, 100 m descent, gradients otherwise negligible
Food and drink Grassington, Kettlewell, Starbotton (500 m offroute), Buckden (300 m offroute)
Summary riverside paths as far as Grassington, then a dramatic traverse of limestone uplands with open views into Wharfedale and Littondale before descent to the Wharfe

13·2	3·3		3·2		3·0		4·3	27·0
Burnsall		5·3 Grassington		5·1 Conistone Pie		4·8 Kettlewell		6·9 Buckden

- From Burnsall Bridge, continue upstream on the path, wheelchair-friendly at first, with the River Wharfe on your right, passing two impressive limestone scars (Wilfrid and Loup) around mile 13·5.

- Beyond the accessible section, the Way climbs and passes through woodland, and at mile 14·2 reaches Hebden suspension bridge. Originally created by a local blacksmith over a century ago, this wire and steel structure sways disconcertingly on a windy day, but it has been reconstructed strongly and is safe.

Loup Scar, from the Way

- Turn left beside the river along a lovely section where its still waters run deep, and an avenue of chestnut trees frames the path.

- At mile 15·6 reach a four-way path junction with a fingerpost 30 m beyond. (These stepping stones could take you across the Wharfe to Linton Church, dating from the 12th century and known as the 'Cathedral of the Dales'.)

River Wharfe at mile 13·8

- Go ahead on a driveway past Riverside Grange and other large houses. Where the driveway bends sharply right, turn left through the stile in the stone wall.
- Follow the path across fields, and after 500 m turn right up Sedber Lane, a track framed by stone walls that climbs up to Grassington's embankment.
- Within 450 m reach the B6265 (Hebden Road) and turn left, passing (or visiting) the National Park Visitor Centre: see page 20.
- About 200 m later, turn right up Main Street and keep ahead through its much-photographed cobbled Square, with several hotels and specialist shops and also the Folk Museum: see the panel opposite.
- Within 300 m reach a junction where you bear left into Chapel Street, past the Methodist Church where you are urged to 'Walk With God': local artist Robert Keep created three panels to connect with walkers on the Dales Way.
- Follow Chapel Street for 270 m, then turn right up Bank Lane, which soon bends left and becomes a walled lane with superb drystone work and fine views. After 200 m, the Way is signed off left for Kettlewell through a gate and across a field to a stile (mile 16·8).

| First, consider the easier option of going ahead through a metal gate to stay on Bank Lane: follow this traditional track for 0·6 mile (1 km) to rejoin the Way at mile 17·5. If you are carrying a heavy pack, avoiding several stiles may make this option attractive: skip the next bullet.

Welcome to Grassington

- Otherwise, go left across a narrow field down to a gated stile. Go uphill to another stile near the far left corner of the next field. Go ahead with a wall on your right. The path curves left to go through two gaps in adjacent walls and continues with the wall on your right.
- The path now leads onto rough pasture and is soon joined by the unofficial route. Start to enjoy wide open views over boulder-studded limestone landscape.
- Behind you, at 506 m (1660 ft), Burnsall Fell towers over the grassy limestone slopes of Elbolton and Kail Hill. Ignore all paths to the left, and go straight ahead on a trod path until you reach a wall which you cross by this gap-stile.
- Beneath your feet are the remains of the medieval settlement of Lea Green. A mile to your right, hidden by the hills, are abandoned lead mines. Cresting the rise of Lea Green, an almost lunar landscape appears, with limestone outcrops and pavement.

Gap-stile leading to Lea Green

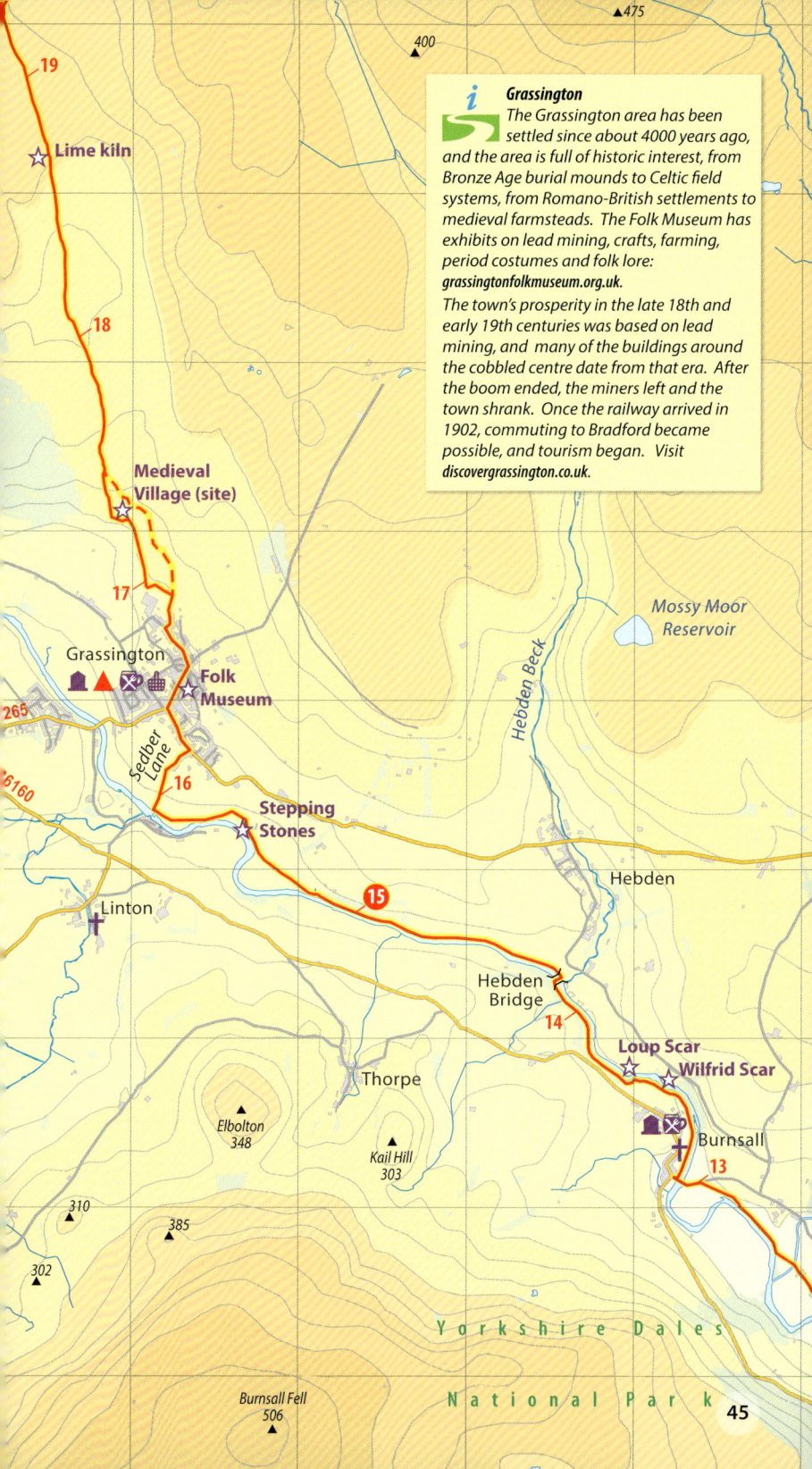

Restored lme kiln at mile 18·7

- Go through the wall and follow the well-defined path through two more walls. Climb gently through a shallow valley past a restored lime kiln on the left at mile 18·7.
- Keep ahead past the lime kiln, slightly west of north on a path that varies between faintly trod and a broad grassy road. Ignore all turnings to the left, including a couple that branch off left to Conistone.
- Pass above Conistone Dib, the steep-sided limestone gorge where climbers sometime practise. Continue through the gate to cross the road (Scot Gate Lane) diagonally to the left. A fingerpost promises Kettlewell in 3 miles.
- Follow a broad track with a limestone scar and scree slope on your right. Cross a wall and at mile 19·7, pass (or climb) Conistone Pie – a natural limestone feature that looks almost manmade. From 350 m (1150 ft) above sea level, enjoy fine views over Kilnsey Crag, Littondale and Wharfedale.

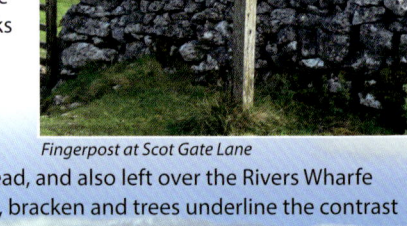

Fingerpost at Scot Gate Lane

- The descent to Kettlewell is long and gentle, offering lovely views – distant ahead, and also left over the Rivers Wharfe and Skirfare. Lower down, grazing sheep, bracken and trees underline the contrast with the arid high ground that you just crossed.
- After crossing four more walls you pass a cairn and descend slightly towards the corner of a stone wall. Keep the wall to your left, and pass through a gate and some trees.

Conistone Pie: a superb viewpoint

Fox & Hounds, Starbotton

War memorial, Kettlewell

47

- At mile 21, bear left to descend steeply on Highgate Leys Lane (a gravel track) to meet Conistone Lane, a road where you turn right.
- After 600 m on the narrow public road, turn right through a small gate signed Kettlewell 5/8 mile, but be aware that you face nine stiles and five gates over the next half mile. If heading for Kettlewell Camping, you may prefer to stay on Conistone Lane for a further 700 m.
- The Way leaves the road to cross two fields and pass through a gate on your right. Continue with the wall at first on your left, then cross it several times.
- At a fingerpost, turn left into a walled lane that adjoins many back gardens in Kettlewell. At the end, turn right past Fold Farm, then left at the narrow road (Scabbate Gate).
- Pass the Kings Head pub (open Wednesdays to Sundays in 2025) on the right, and within 80 m bear right into Middle Lane, soon passing a war memorial.
- After 150 m, Middle Lane makes a T-junction with the B6160, opposite a car park with public toilets. Turn left to cross the River Wharfe again.
- On the far side of the bridge, turn sharp right down shallow steps to the stony footpath. Follow the river bank to a kissing-gate leading through National Trust land in Upper Wharfedale, and follow the riverside path upstream.
- Pass through a classic Dales landscape of field and barn with stretches of walled lane. The path generally occupies the narrow margin between river and the slopes up to the fells. Don't be led astray by broad vehicle tracks heading through gates that may stand open: look instead for the waymarked footpath over stiles.
- At mile 24·8 a footbridge leads across towards Starbotton and you may want to detour to the Fox & Hounds Inn. The flood monitoring apparatus attached to the footbridge reminds us that the Wharfe can be a powerful river.
- The Way stays west of the river, which soon bends away across the flood plain for nearly a mile. Meanwhile the Way goes through gates and over stiles to cross fields, passing various barns and crossing Step Gill by a footbridge. In places it reduces to a narrow path enclosed between stone walls.
- At mile 26·1, after passing a barn the Way rises to join a broad former carriage drive below Birks Wood. Follow it for 500 m, then look for the fingerpost pointing you right through a gate to descend a narrow path towards the river.
- Keep right along the field edge to reach the river embankment, and follow it for 900 m to reach a road, Dubb's Lane. For the Buck Inn and other facilities in Buckden, turn right at mile 27 and cross the river.
- To continue the Way, cross the road diagonally to the left via gates and continue beside the river.

Descend a narrow path to the river at mile 26·5

3.4 Buckden to Cowgill

| | 49 | 51 | 56 | 57 |

Distance 17.7 miles 28.5 km
Terrain well-defined field paths, farm tracks, moorland rising to 520 m/1700 ft, roads (27%)
Grade steadily rising path with steeper section beyond Swarthghyll, altitude gain 300 m; steady descent 200 m to Far Gearstones; steady ascent 100 m then steeper descent of 200 m from Dent Head Viaduct
Food and drink Hubberholme, Ribblehead (2.3 km offroute), Cowgill (Sportsmans Inn)
Summary lovely riverside walks, a scenic high-level hike in Yorkshire's Three Peaks country, views over the famous Settle-Carlisle railway, ending in the sheltered paths of Dentdale

27.0 — 5.1 — 4.4 — 3.0 — 5.2 — 44.7
Buckden — 8.2 — Beckermonds — 7.1 — Cam Houses — 4.8 — Far Gearstones — 8.4 — Cowgill

- At mile 27, ignore the track leading ahead to the road. Instead, turn right along a recently constructed path that clings to the river, staying away from the traffic.

- After 600 m, the path turns left away from the river to reach Dubb's Lane. Emerge through this gate and turn right (unsigned) for the final 300 m of road into Hubberholme.

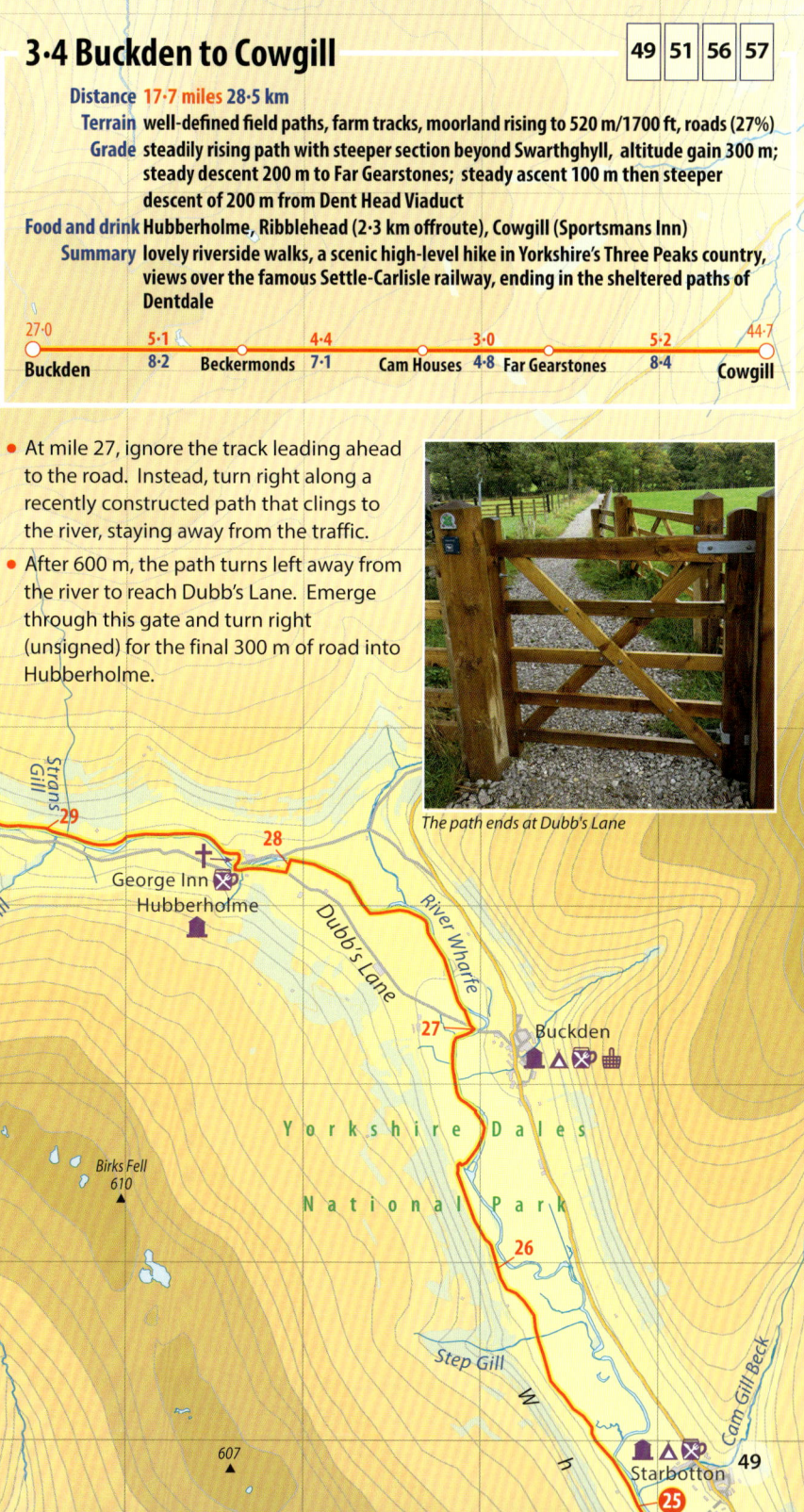

The path ends at Dubb's Lane

The George Inn, Hubberholme

- Reach, and perhaps visit, the George Inn (B&B and meals from 12 noon from Wednesday to Sunday in 2025). This traditional pub celebrates its connection with the writer and broadcaster J B Priestley (1894-1984).

- Just across the river, visit the medieval church of St Michael & All Angels Church. Hubberholme was Priestley's favourite place and he and his wife Jacquetta Hawkes had their ashes buried in its graveyard: see the panel.

- After the church, follow the path upstream, now on the right bank of the river. In places it is very rocky and narrow, sometimes grassy, punctuated by stiles and gates. Cross Strans Gill by a footbridge at mile 28·9.

> **Hubberholme Church**
> The Norman church of St Michael and All Angels crouches beside the river, as if sheltering from the wind.
> Its outstanding feature is its oak rood loft. This is a wooden gallery designed to support a cross, and it dates from 1558. Many such adornments were destroyed during the 16th and 17th centuries: this is a rare survivor. Oak pews by Robert Thompson bear his carved mouse trademark, which you may recognise from St Peter's if you visited it: see page 37.

St Michael and All Angels, Hubberholme

- Stay close to the river until mile 29·7, then before a farmyard turn right up to a stile over a wall. Turn left to a gate and emerge through a further gate. Continue in front of the large farmhouse at Yockenthwaite.
- Ignore the access road over the arched bridge to your left. Stay high to locate a gate among the trees. Follow a farm track close to the river, passing a small lime kiln and stone circle.

Yockenthwaite

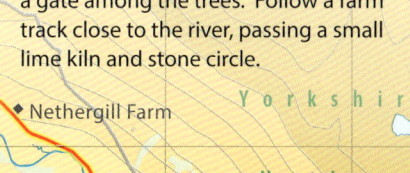

Bronze Age stone circle at mile 30·4

Beckermonds

- Approaching a ruined barn with an asymmetrical roofline, veer right on a path that rises to a gap in the wall. Continue across the field, go through a stile and turn right.
- Follow the wall around the field to reach a point opposite the stile. Cross Deepdale Gill by footbridge below Deepdale Farm, on your right.
- Turn left to the public road and cross the Wharfe by Deepdale Bridge. Immediately turn right beside the river on a broad and uneven track that leads towards Beckermonds.
- After New House Farm, the track rises and narrows, eventually taking you over a stile and up to gates. Turn right to cross the footbridge over Green Field Beck and follow the walled lane up to Beckermonds and a minor road at mile 32.
- Turn right along the road, which within 200 m climbs to the junction with another road. Turn left (unsigned), steeply uphill at first, towards the bleak grandeur of the fells.
- Follow this road to and through Oughtershaw, with its marker stone. At mile 33·2, the main road bears right and climbs: leave it here, turning off left on a vehicle track. The engraved wall signs announce this as the private access road to Nethergill and Swarthghyll Farms.

Marker stone, Oughtershaw

- Follow the curved valley of Oughtershaw Beck, passing Nethergill Farm (self-catering, drinks and snacks) at mile 33·9. After nearly a mile (1·5 km) reach Swarthghyll Farm (Walkers' Flats, meals by arrangement) along the rough private road with grassy middle.
- Approach a shelter band of trees and pass between two pillars marking the entrance to the farm. To continue the Way, turn left before the courtyard through a metal gate – or, if staying at Swarthghyll, enter the courtyard on the right.

South-east over Breadpiece Barn

- Exit Swarthghyll through gates passing a long barn and emerging onto open moorland. The path meanders and is boggy or muddy in places, but always well defined.
- Pass through some recent plantation of trees, straddling streams. Where the wall on your left ends, continue beside a fence. Afterwards, pass though a wall and cross Far End Gill to approach Far End Barn, keeping it on your left.
- At the next barn (Breadpiece) the fingerpost turns you right through the wall, and then go left for a few metres. Climb right over a ladder stile and decrepit wall.
- Cross Grainings Gill to another ladder-stile and another decrepit wall. Your destination (Cam Houses) soon comes into view. If its Snow-Trac vehicle is still in use, ideally suited to traversing boggy ground, you will see it from afar.
- Cross a ladder stile to pass in front of the first house. Turn right through a gate, then left on the farm access road. Go left through a metal gate, then turn right in front of the barns.

East over Cam Houses from the Way

- If you intend to switch to the Watershed Alternatives, skip to page 81. Otherwise, turn left down to and through a gate with fingerpost, and follow a narrow, muddy walled lane.
- Cross the small field towards the right corner of the conifer plantation. The path is indistinct in places, and crosses several small streams. Ignore the gate in the wall on your right. Cross the plantation corner on the signed path.
- Cross a vehicle track and climb diagonally to a stone cairn on the skyline where you join Cam High Road, built by the Romans in AD 80. It is shared with the Pennine Way which joins you from the right.
- At just over 520 m/1700 ft above sea level, this is the highest point on the main Dales Way. The scenery is dominated by Yorkshire's Three Peaks: see the panel.

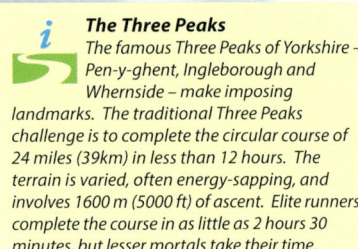

The Three Peaks
The famous Three Peaks of Yorkshire – Pen-y-ghent, Ingleborough and Whernside – make imposing landmarks. The traditional Three Peaks challenge is to complete the circular course of 24 miles (39km) in less than 12 hours. The terrain is varied, often energy-sapping, and involves 1600 m (5000 ft) of ascent. Elite runners complete the course in as little as 2 hours 30 minutes, but lesser mortals take their time.

- Go left, descending steadily to Cam End at mile 38·4, with another cairn and marker post. Bear slightly right, ignoring the Pennine Way and Bridleway which fork left (south). On a clear day you can spot the Ribblehead Viaduct about 5 km (3 miles) to the south-west.
- Continue down another section of Roman road, and at mile 39·3 cross Gayle Beck by a footbridge. Pass through a gate with fingerpost and turn left up a broad, stony vehicle track. (Gayle Beck soon joins the Ribble, eventually to flow into the Irish Sea, confirming that you have crossed the watershed.)
- After 170 m, the track reaches a gate/cattle grid and you emerge at the main road. Take care of fast-moving traffic when you cross the B6255. From mile 39·5 the Way continues north on a tarmac lane signed for Shepherds Cottage, with fingerpost 'Dent Head 2½'.
- If staying at Ribblehead (Station Inn and Gauber Bunk Barn), do not leave the road yet. Instead turn left (west) along the north verge of the busy road for 1·5 miles (2·4 km), taking care to see and be seen. Retrace your steps next day to turn left (north) up the track.

Cam High Road

- If staying at Shepherds Cottage (B&B with evening meals by arrangement), go ahead up its tarmac lane for 500 m. Steps on your left lead to its wooden gate. Skip the next bullet.
- Just before reaching Shepherds Cottage, turn off its tarmac lane at the two-bladed fingerpost on the left. Follow the leftmost blade up a grassy sloping path.
- Continue steeply uphill on a narrow, sodden path that turns right about 150 m past the farmhouse to converge with a stone wall to its right. The terrain can be extremely boggy. Look behind you for possible views of Pen-y-Ghent and Ingleborough.

South-west from the path towards Ingleborough

- Keep beside the wall for over half a mile (850 m), crossing a couple of stiles. After High Gayle, keep ahead where the wall turns right downhill. At mile 40·6, bear slightly left at a fingerpost.
- You now follow Black Rake Road, a historic track which joins from below on the right. It is mainly stony or grassy, but boggy in places. Look behind you for distant views of Pen-y-ghent.
- The track rises at first, then descends gently to meet Dent Road at mile 41·8. Bear left along the road, joined by the Watershed Alternative from Newby Head Gate.
- Aye Gill Pike and Baugh Fell loom on the skyline, and far ahead you might glimpse the Scafell range. Follow the road, soon sighting ahead some of the ten arches of Dent Head Viaduct on the Settle-Carlisle railway, see page 23. At mile 42·6, the Way passes under it.
- Over the next section, the road runs closely beside the Dee to mile 43·7. As of early 2026, this road was still closed to walkers, as well as to vehicles, by repair works on a major landslip. Check for Route updates at *www.rucsacs.com/books/daw*.
- Dent Head Viaduct is a scheduled Ancient Monument, built in 1869-75 from local dark limestone known as Dent Marble. For a closer look, once across the river detour right off the road.

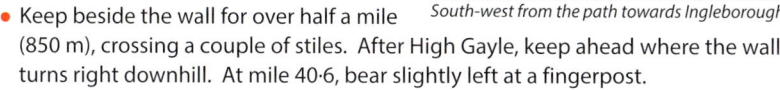

Dent Head Viaduct from the Way

- About 300 m later, pass Bridge End Cottage, which once housed a hand knitting school for local people. Nearby, a gate leads to a riverside picnic area with a sign welcoming Dales Way walkers.
- At mile 43·7, the road bends sharply left to cross the River Dee by the narrow Stone House Bridge. Look back right up the cul-de-sac to Arten Gill Viaduct, another Ancient Monument built from Dent Marble. The Watershed Alternative from Arten Gill Moss rejoins the Way here: see page 84.
- You reach the Sportsman's Inn at mile 44·2 (B&B and refreshments from 16.00 on most weekdays in 2025). The road gives good views over the limestone river bed, sculpted into interesting forms by fast-moving water. When in spate, the river runs rapidly, but sometimes in summer, when the water table is low, it stays underground.
- After several miles of road-walking, the section ends at mile 44·7 where the final Watershed Alternative (down the Coal Road, see page 85) rejoins the Way at Lea Yeat Bridge.

Packhorse bridge dwarfed by Dent Head Viaduct

Lee Yeat Bridge

3·5 Cowgill to Sedbergh

		59	60	62	63

Distance 12·7 miles 20·4 km
Terrain field paths, not always well-defined, farm tracks, roads (17%)
Grade gently undulating with ascent and descent of 70 m between Dentdale and Millthrop
Food and drink Dent (pubs and café) and Sedbergh (wide choice, 900 m offroute)
Summary beautiful valley walking with wide views of the surrounding hills, featuring the contrasting attractions of Dent and Sedbergh

```
44·7         4·1              4·9              3·7        57·4
●────────────●────────────────●────────────────●──────────●
Cowgill      6·6    Dent      7·9   Millthrop  6·0   Sedbergh
```

- Ignore Lea Yeat Bridge, by which the road crosses the river at mile 45. Instead go ahead offroad through a gate, staying on the south bank. Follow a narrow, rocky path festooned with tree roots for 530 m to Ewegales Bridge.

- Don't cross the bridge, but join the minor road, on the south bank. After 420 m bear left up a broad track (its fingerpost hidden in this 2025 photo) for Laithbank at mile 45·3.

- Cross the sloping pasture, heading towards Rivling's farm buildings on a path that may be awash. Stay below the farm to enter Little Town, a replanted woodland area, over a step-stile. Exit the woodland, descend steps to cross a driveway to cottages, and cross a second small area of trees.

- Emerge from the trees and look ahead for your first views of Dent. A gate leads to the access track to Hackergill Farm where you turn left and then right on a lane to cross Hacker Gill, then cross the paved drive of the Coat Faw mansion.

Ahead towards Dent after emerging from the trees

Bear left for Laithbank: see page 58 bullet 2

- Follow signs carefully around the back of a cottage at Clint and in front of West Clint Farm, crossing pastures, heading almost west and maintaining a steady altitude.
- Descend to cross Stock Beck by footbridge and bear right down the lane near Laithbank to the public road to Dent. Turn left briefly along it at mile 46·7.
- After 220 m of road, just past Tub Hole (a house), turn right down a footpath and descend a field to cross a tree-lined ravine called Lenny's Leap. Go over stiles to a narrow, almost hidden footbridge (Nelly Bridge) over the River Dee.
- On its far side, turn left to follow the riverbank for 650 m over stiles across four fields to reach Tommy Bridge. This substantial footbridge is surprisingly easy to miss: look on your left for a gate with fingerpost to cross over.
- Once across, immediately turn right through a gate and down steps to follow the riverbank past a ford. Near the field corner, look for a half-hidden gate-stile into the next field.
- Bear left to cross this field diagonally up and over a hillock at mile 47·6, heading towards a large beech tree which has a nearby post with yellow marker.

Waymarker post at mile 47·6

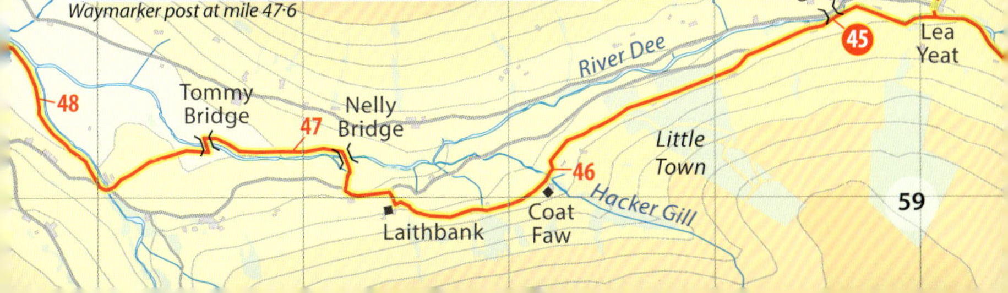

- Maintain the same heading (south-west) and descend to the next marker post at the corner of a stone wall. Exit by a wooden gate to bear right across the road bridge.
- Within 30 metres of road, turn right through a small gate and drop down to a riverside path signed 'Church Bridge 1 mile'. In places, erosion has eaten away at the bank and care is needed.
- After 700 m beside Deepdale Beck and several gates, the beck joins the River Dee at mile 48·2. From here on, the valley floor is wide and flat, and the Way follows the flood embankment.
- After 800 m beside the Dee, punctuated mainly by gates, veer left around a field corner and cross Keld Beck by concrete footbridge.
- Turn right through a metal kissing-gate and pass Dent's football pitches to approach the road across Church Bridge. Steps lead up to two very narrow squeeze-stiles – suitable mainly for those with very long, thin legs.
- Most people will anyway wish to detour into Dent village: bear left along a path and keep ahead uphill on the road for 300 m: see page 61 for Dent's attractions.
- Afterwards, either retrace your steps to Church Bridge or continue along the Laning (road) past the Heritage Centre. Within 400 m you will rejoin the Way, and after 80 m on the road, bear right (signed for Barth Bridge) on a footpath beside the fields. Skip to page 63.

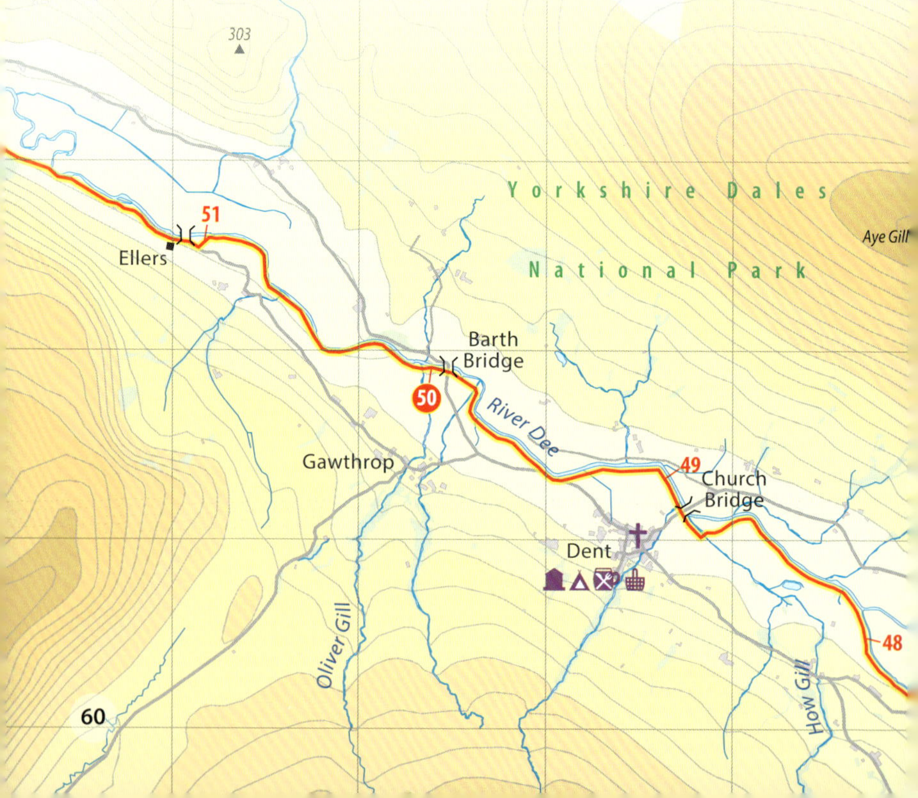

Deepdale Beck around mile 48·1

Dent village and Dentdale

Dentdale resembles a Yorkshire dale in miniature. It has been occupied since ancient times, with farms above the marshy valley floor, but close to springs. In recent times, fields below the farms have been improved, whilst the land above remains as rough grazing.

Dent village clusters around its cobbled streets and St Andrew's Parish Church, dating from the 12th century. A medieval fair held in June drew people back home every year for a week of sports and celebration. Dent established its own grammar school early in the 17th century.

The Sun Inn, Dent

Hand-knitting was at the heart of the Dentdale economy in the 17th and 18th centuries, rising to a peak during the Napoleonic Wars. Everyone knitted at a furious pace as they went about their daily business, even while walking about or doing their chores. The dexterity and energy of Dent's 'terrible knitters' is explained in the Heritage Centre. Schools were set up to teach knitting, not only to children, but also to workers who were building the railway.

Dent Marble, a fossil-rich black limestone, was quarried at Arten Gill. It was used for a wide range of purposes from railway viaducts to a fireplace for the Tsar's Winter Palace in St Petersburg. In the late 19th century, cheap Italian imports forced it off the market.

For more about Dentdale, visit its Museum and Heritage Centre which is open daily year-round from 9.00 (with variable closing times): tel 01539 625 800. The main museum has exhibits on farming, slavery, the railway and famous sons of Dent including Adam Sedgwick: see page 21. It also houses a tearoom and the Woolshed, where a video explains the creation of handcrafted woollen products from sheep to garment, with examples on sale: **www.dentvillageheritagecentre.com**.

Dent Museum and Heritage Centre

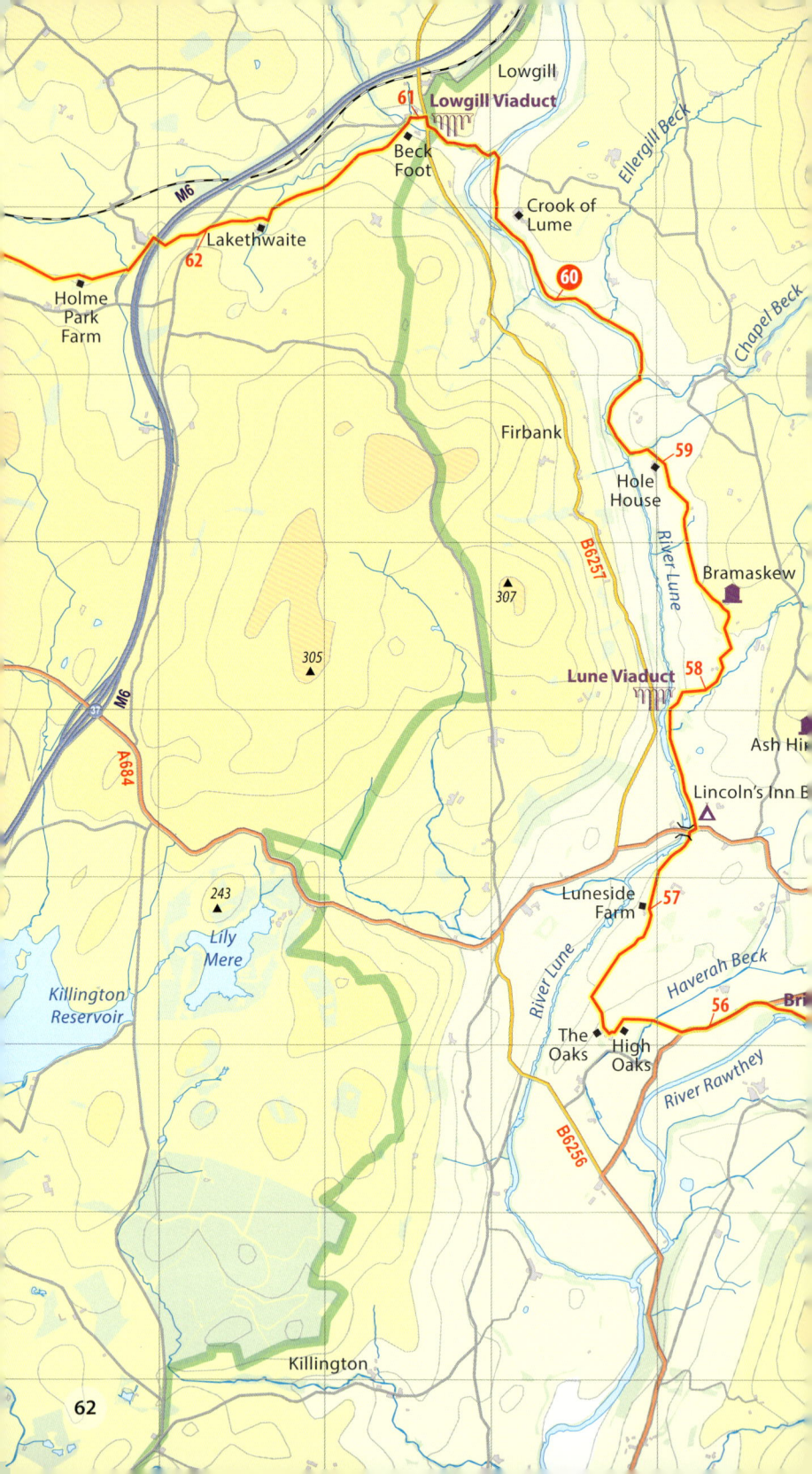

- After Dent, continue beside the river from Church Bridge, after 900 m reaching a short stretch beside the public road at mile 49·4. After just 80 m leave the road on a riverside footpath signed for Barth Bridge, which you reach at mile 50.
- Don't cross the river here: that's where the Dales High Way goes. Remain instead on its south bank, climbing steps to cross over the road bridge. The field narrows and a sign points left towards a stile and a lane.
- At mile 51, turn right along the lane to and past Ellers Farm, and a mile later reach Brackensgill. Follow the track on the right and turn left to cross the footbridge, returning to the track once across the River Dee.

The path to Barth Bridge

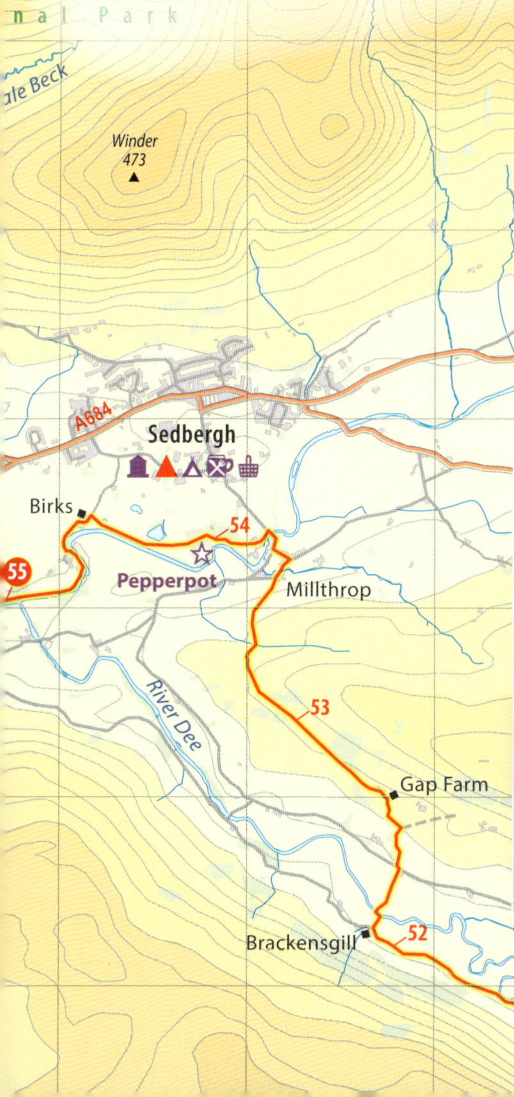

Footbridge across the River Dee near Ellers

- After your final crossing of the Dee, continue ahead up the narrow lane to reach and cross a minor road. Continue on Gap Lane (signed Millthrop) beside a high stone wall, passing Gate Cottage. After 200 m the lane forks: turn left.
- Pass Gap Farm on your right, and go through a gate, across a field and through Gap Wood. Now follow a green bridleway for about 600 m, staying close to a wall on your right. Sedbergh comes into view with the Howgill Fells as backdrop.
- Go through a gate and descend straight ahead. The path soon joins a vehicle track that descends to the road at Millthrop. Turn right, then after 120 m turn left down to the road to Sedbergh.

The Way turns left, signed for Birks

- Turn right to cross the River Rawthey by Millthrop Bridge. To visit Sedbergh, continue ahead beside the road for 900 m with great care: the road has no verge for the first 500 m. To continue the Way, immediately turn left on a footpath signed for Birks, soon crossing woodland.

Sedbergh

Pronounced sed-ber, the town sits at the foot of the Howgill Fells. The name comes from the Old Norse for flat-topped hill. St Andrew's Church and Sedbergh's motte and bailey castle dominated the settlement in the 12th century. Its famous public (independent) school was founded in 1525, and has become the town's largest employer: **sedberghschool.org**.

Sedbergh's Quaker heritage is strong, dating from 1652 when George Fox preached outside St Andrew's Church to a large crowd for several hours: see page 32.

Traditional industries were sheep farming and hand-knitting, in the 20th century augmented by tourism. The outbreak of foot and mouth disease in 2001 severely affected the local economy, and in 2006 Sedbergh reinvented itself as England's Book Town, joining Hay-on-Wye (Wales) and Wigtown (Scotland). For more, including lists of annual festival events, visit **www.sedbergh.org.uk**

St Andrew's Church, Sedbergh

- Exit the wood near its end by a kissing-gate on the right, passing the 'Pepperpot' folly (restored in 2015 by Sedbergh School). Descend through a large gap in a stone wall, go through a wooden kissing-gate and continue beside the River Rawthey to reach a narrow road at Birks (mile 54·6).
- Turn left along the road and follow its double-bend. To detour to the Quaker Meetinghouse at Brigflatts, turn right off-road through the kissing-gate in the hedge on the right, signed 'Brigflatts': see page 32.
- To continue the Way, stay on Birks Lane and after 250 m, turn off it to resume the riverside path, soon passing sewage works on your right.
- Climb steps to cross the disused railway embankment at mile 55·3 and continue beside the river to the A683. You pass near Brigflatts at mile 55·6, but can't visit it unless you detour as above.
- Turn left along the A683, and at a marker post after 550 m, cross the road with care and head through the wooden kissing-gate opposite, signed for High Oaks. Cross Haverah Beck to a signpost pointing the Way over the shoulder of a hill.
- Cross the field diagonally to its far corner, then turn left on a hedge-lined track at mile 56·4. At High Oaks, follow signs between the buildings, and leave along another hedge-lined track.
- Where this track ends, turn right to a gate at the end of the field. Continue beside the hedge, and go left through a gate to Luneside Farm.
- A prominent sign turns you left through a pedestrian gate. Follow the field edge to cross a stile. Descend to approach the banks of the River Lune, heading towards Lincoln's Inn Bridge. This dates from the 17th century, named after the inn-keeper Lincoln whose tavern pre-dated it.
- Go up to the road and turn right along it for 30 metres, then turn left down the track signed for Low Branthwaite. There's a campsite and limited accommodation nearby, and the centre of Sedbergh is 1·8 miles (2·9 km) to the east by the A684.

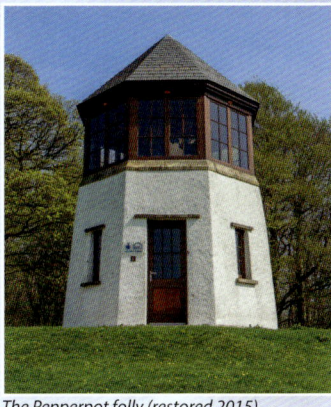

The Pepperpot folly (restored 2015)

Lincoln's Inn Bridge

3·6 Sedbergh to Burneside

Distance	12·3 miles 19·8 km
Terrain	field paths, often undefined, farm tracks, roads (18%)
Grade	gentle undulations, no major ascents or descents
Food and drink	Kendal (wide choice, 2·9 km offroute), Burneside
Summary	attractive walking north in the Lune valley, then west with intricate navigation on twisting, undulating paths through fields, ending in the valley of the River Kent

57·4 Sedbergh — 4·8 / 7·7 — M6 — 4·1 / 6·6 — Black Moss Tarn — 3·4 / 6·0 — 69·7 Burneside

- From Lincoln's Inn Bridge, the Way goes upstream beside the River Lune, past its rapids and through its woodland. After 600 m, climb a ladder-stile and turn right to cross the footbridge over Crosdale Beck.
- Pass under the Lune Viaduct, a Grade II Listed structure built by the Lancaster & Carlisle Railway from red sandstone.
- Turn right uphill to a marker post. After 40 m a fingerpost points across the field. Go through the gate in the corner, looking towards the Howgills.
- Walk beside a fence to cross the Low Branthwaite access track to a stile, and continue up the field on a curving trod path, passing hawthorn hedges: see the photo opposite.

The Lune Viaduct

Cross the field to the corner gate

The Way follows a curving trod path uphill

- Go through a wooden gate ahead, continuing uphill on a path with a stone wall on the left, towards a tall, spreading tree.
- At the gate shown below into Bramaskew Farm, bear left towards a large ash tree. Go through the stone wall by a gate-stile to its right. Walk with the telegraph wires to your left, then cross a ladder-stile.
- Head towards a small barn, which you pass to its left. Continue towards the end of a wall, which you keep on your right. Leave the field by a lane. Just before an ancient barn, go left into a field and turn right.
- At the corner, a fingerpost directs you downhill to Hole House, following the wall on your right to a metal gate. Go through the gate and over a hill.
- Descend to Hole House farmyard and go between the two houses. Cross Smithy Beck and turn left to reach the River Lune at mile 59·2.
- Keep closely beside the river for the next 1·2 miles (1·9 km), crossing Chapel Beck and Ellergill Becks by footbridges and climbing a few stiles. Take great care on the path above the river: erosion has narrowed it significantly.
- At mile 60·4, emerge from Crook of Lune Wood and follow the signpost to turn right uphill through a gate, away from the river. Traffic noise from the M6 ahead becomes obvious, and Lowgill Viaduct appears to the left.

The gate into Bramaskew Farm

67

Crook of Lune Bridge, Lowgill

- Ignore a farm track on the right, and at the public road turn left. Cross the river by Crook of Lune Bridge, a narrow, delicate crossing still bearing light traffic.
- Walk uphill and after 400 m or so pass under Lowgill Viaduct, another fine red sandstone legacy of the Lancaster & Carlisle Railway. At the T-junction, turn right and after 60 m turn left along the Old Scotch Road to Beckfoot.
- After 90 m look for an easily missed turning left uphill, passing left of a white cottage (Half Island House) onto a hedge-lined narrow footpath.
- Where the hedge turns left, continue ahead for 250 m, then turn left uphill to the field corner. Look behind you for views back over the viaduct and the Howgills beyond, with the River the Lune down to your left.
- Cross a wire fence and continue parallel to the M6. Continue through the gate and turn left to an access road towards Lakethwaite Farm. At mile 61·8, just before the farm, go right, over a stile.
- Go uphill diagonally to cross onto a farm track. Go right at first, then veer left to reach another stile in the corner of the field. Look behind you for views over the Howgills.
- Exit onto the road (the Old Scotch Road again) and turn left briefly. After 80 m, at a fingerpost turn right across a stone wall with steps. Walk to a gate and continue across the field, bearing down left to a muddy patch before the gate leading to the M6 footbridge (Lambrigg Head).

Muddy patch leading to the M6 footbridge

Lowgill Viaduct

- Once across the motorway, turn sharp left to pass the farm on your right. Follow the road for a bit further than the 200 m stated by the wooden sign, ready to turn right into a field, down some steps, over a footbridge and through a gate.
- Follow a wall to the left to reach and go through a gate in the field corner. Continue across another field to a timber stile, then along a narrow lane past Holme Park Farm.
- Cross a stile (ramshackle in 2025) and continue along the edge of the next field with a hedge on your right. Exit by stone steps, then bear half-right to a gate. Go diagonally across more fields (mostly by waymarked stiles) maintaining a north-westerly direction.
- Exit the last field by a gate to a narrow fenced path which crosses a stream and passes in front of Morsedale Hall.
- Cross a lane near Hardrigg and follow a fence on your right to reach the green metal railway fence. Turn left beside the West Coast mainline for 200 m including a ladder-stile.
- Exit by large metal gate to cross the railway by road bridge and immediately turn left down steps to a lineside footpath.

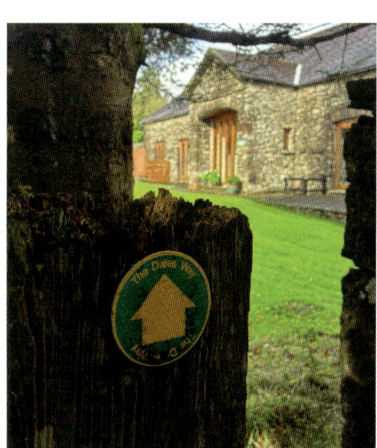

Pass in front of Morsedale Hall

| Alternatively, should you need to visit Grayrigg (e.g. for a bus to Kendal), go ahead on the lane for 1 km. To resume the Way from here, turn left beside the A685 for 900 m, then turn off right at the Animal Rescue Cumbria and follow a path for 320 m to resume the Way at mile 64·8. Skip to bullet 3 on page 70.

Turn right to descend a trod path at mile 63·9

- Otherwise, from the road bridge keep beside the railway for 450 m, then turn right downhill on the trod path shown above. In case the path isn't clear enough, the grid reference is 575 961. Aim north, descending to the left of the trees by this stream, between two small hills.
- Turn left along a farm road to pass around Green Head Farm, passing through signed gates with two double-bends. At mile 64·6 cross Lambrigg Beck by footbridge, go through Grayrigg Foot farmyard and cross straight over the A685 with care.
- In the field, turn right to join a farm road which bears left. After the bridge over Thrushgill Beck, turn left across a field and follow a faint path curving right to a gate in the field top corner.
- Don't go through the gate, but follow the fence on your left and join a vehicle track that bends right. Before a ruined stone building, bear left and descend to a footbridge over the River Mint.
- Continue to a gate into a lane lined with hedgerow, a haven for small birds and tiny mammals. Follow the lane for about 300 m, turning right into the access road to Shaw End, a 19th century mansion.

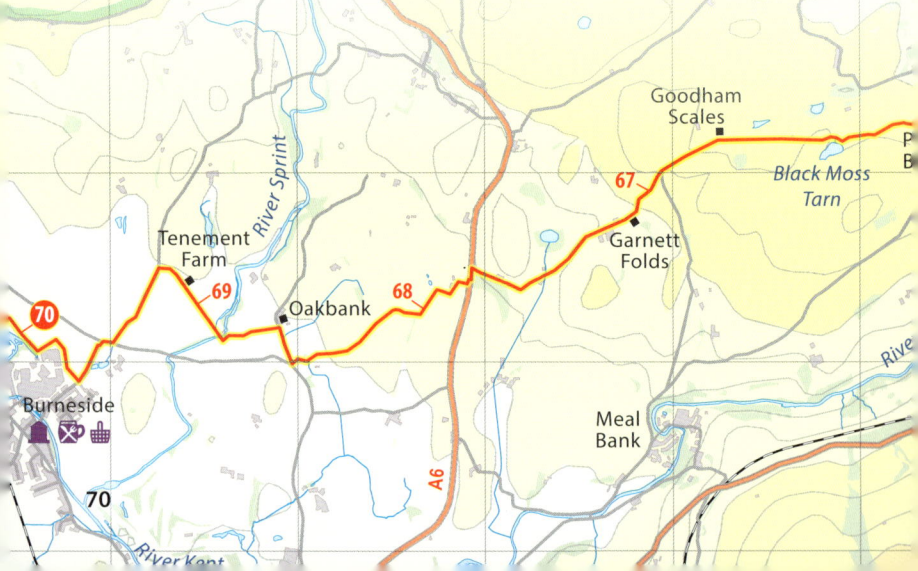

Kissing-gate up the bank on the left

- Before the lane descends to the mansion, look up the steep bank on the left to turn off left through this timber kissing-gate, in 2025 marked only with a yellow arrow.
- Within 150 m turn left after a stone house called Low Barn and go through a large metal gate to the left of the next house (High Barn). Leave its garden through gates onto a narrow, overgrown path leading within 200 m to a road.
- Cross over the road into a lane signed for Black Moss Tarn. Pass in front of Biglands, seemingly through its garden, then through a narrow field. Enter a larger field, and veer left with a hedge on your left.
- Exit right at a stile and cross a further field along the line of a wall. At a gap in the wall head diagonally down towards Black Moss Tarn and bear right to pass the tarn and perhaps take a closer look at its bird life.

Footbridge across Lambrigg Beck at mile 64·6

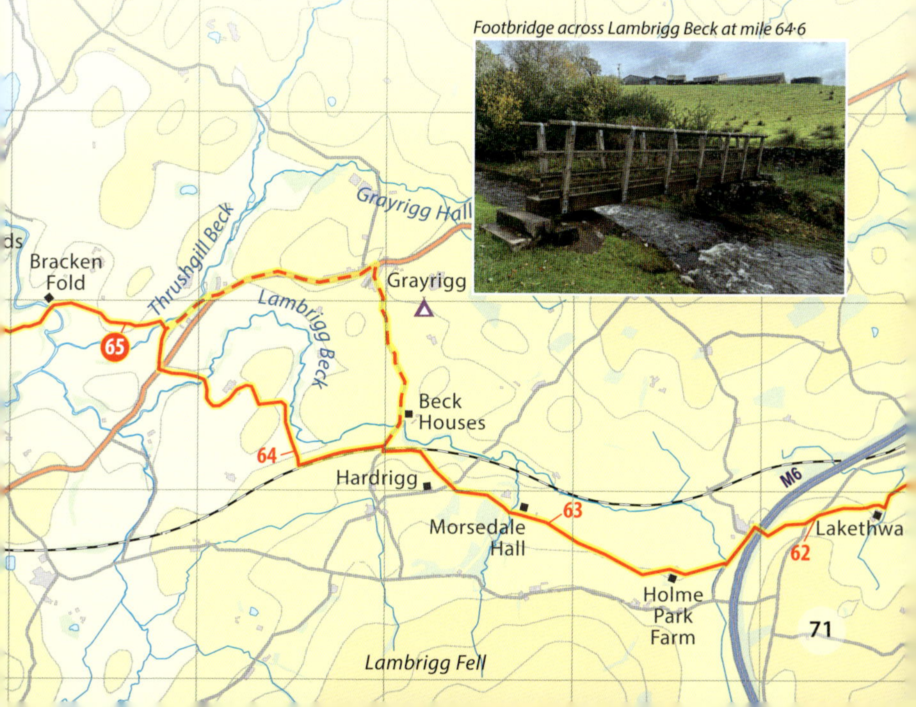

71

- Climb the hill on your right, then descend to an electricity pylon and pass it en route to New House Farm. Cross the cattle grid, keeping the house on your right. Ignore footpaths to the left, and leave by a wooden gate onto a narrow waymarked path.
- At the gate to Goodham Scales continue ahead on the tarmac road. After 250 m take the right (gated) fork and descend for nearly a mile to the A6 at mile 67·7. Turn left to the end of the slip road before crossing this busy road opposite Burton House Farm.
- Go around the farm buildings, passing through gates. Descend to pass a marshy area on your right. Cross a ladder stile, and after 50 m go right at another stile and footbridge. Turn left into a field.
- Follow the hedge on your right until it bends left. Keeping to the left of the field edge, pass through the gate diagonally across another field to a stile.
- Cross the next field, go over a stile and continue with hedge and wall on your left. At the foot of the slope go left over a stile, and descend to a gate. Take the left-hand paved path and emerge at a road junction at mile 68·6.
- Turn right along the road towards Oakbank, and, after 300 m, turn left on a footpath signed Sprint Bridge.
- After 200 m, the path crosses the wall and continues west to the River Sprint. Descend to this footbridge at Sprint Mill, and bear right among buildings through a garden area, to cross a field and pass through gates at Tenement Farm.
- At mile 69·2 the farm access road meets Garnett Bridge Road and you turn left to follow it. After 450 m make a right-left dogleg to continue on Hall Road, soon taking to its fenced footpath on the right.
- After 250 m, you reach a junction with a fingerpost. To continue the Way, turn right (north-west) on a fenced path. For Burneside itself, go straight ahead and cross the River Kent by its Ford Bridge. Completed in 2019, this replaced the one washed away by Storm Desmond.
- To resume the Way after Burneside, cross the Ford Bridge and turn left at the fingerpost at mile 69·7.

River Sprint from the Sprint Mill footbridge

3·7 Burneside to Bowness

74	75	79

Distance 9·9 miles 15·9 km
Terrain well-defined field paths, farm tracks, roads (20%)
Grade a series of climbs and descents totalling 200 m and 250 m respectively
Food and drink Staveley (choice, 600 m offroute), Bowness (wide choice), Windermere station
Summary easy walking beside the River Kent, making a lovely transition to the fringe of the Lake District, and ending at England's largest lake

```
69·7         3·3                 3·7              2·9         79·6
○────────────○───────────────────○────────────────○───────────○
Burneside    5·3    Staveley    6·0              Outrun Nook  4·7  Bowness
```

- From this fingerpost, follow the fenced path around the huge Cropper site, based on the paper mills established in 1845 by James Cropper (1823-1900). He became a Quaker campaigner for landscape conservation, and later a Member of Parliament.

Fingerpost at mile 69·7

- Join the powerful River Kent which, when in spate, can uproot trees. Follow the riverside path to reach and cross Bowston Bridge at mile 70·5. Turn left across the river past the Handsome Brewery, then turn right along the road for 150 m.

- Just after Kent Close (cul-de-sac) turn right at a fingerpost on a narrow path that leads after 800 m to Cowan Head, an upmarket gated community on the site of a former paper mill.

Tree uprooted by the River Kent

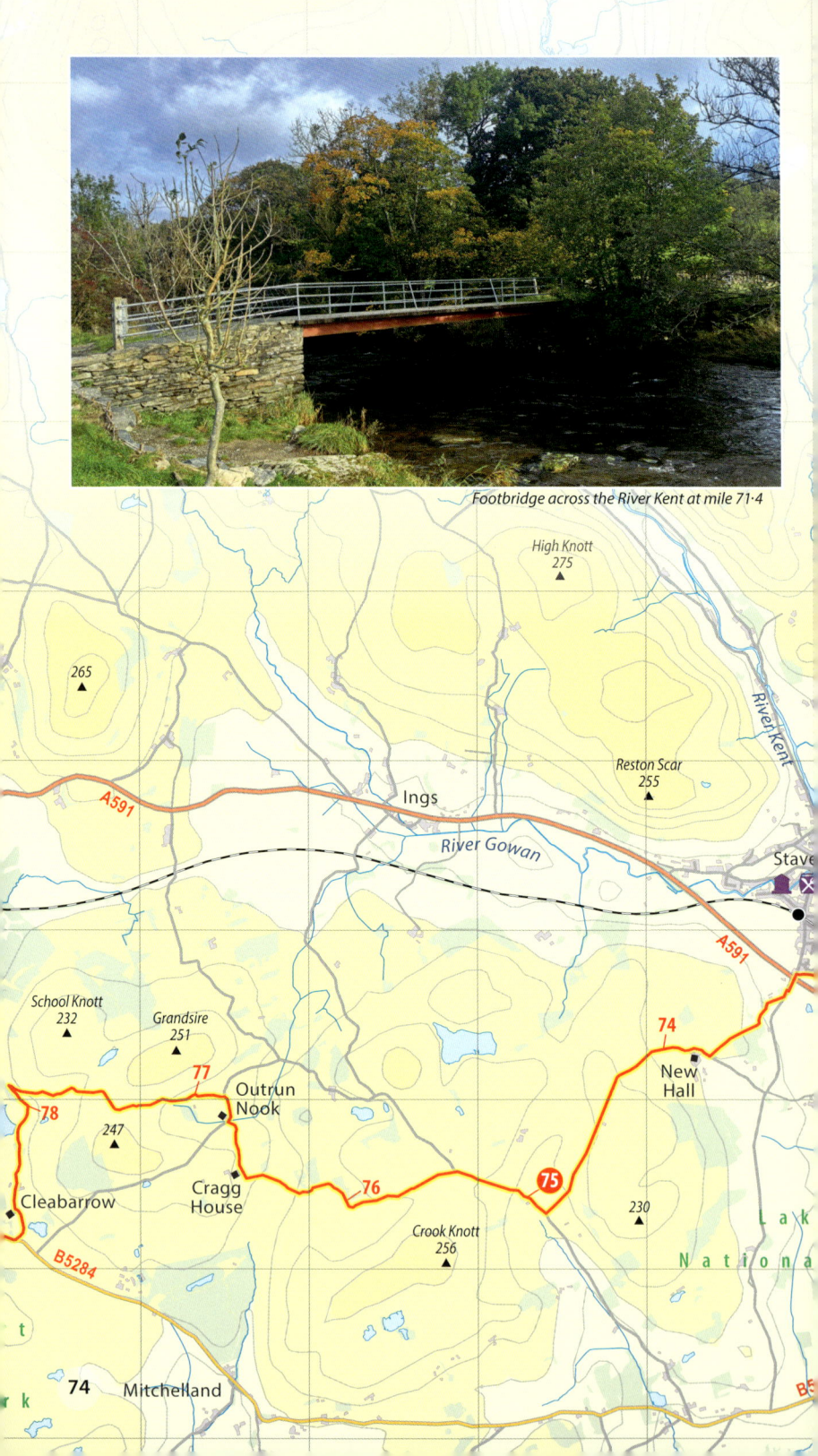
Footbridge across the River Kent at mile 71.4

Tree-lined River Kent at mile 71·7

- Stay on the road that passes to the left of the gated housing, passing more houses and parking, and keep on the path. You have entered the Lake District National Park (see page 25) and the landscape changes. The river bed is rockier, the hillsides more rugged, and there is more woodland.

- Through a gate, the Way remains beside or close to the River Kent for over a mile on a path that may be very muddy and follows the river as it bends westward. At mile 72·6 a fingerpost sends you left (south) for 280 m to meet the Kendal Road.

Water mills
There have been mills along the River Kent since the 13th century, their evolution resembling the mills at Addingham, Linton and Sedbergh. Changing needs, opportunities and economic competition all created changes in how mills worked. Many began by grinding corn but later sharpened blades, sawed timber, made and processed woollen and cotton goods and ground animal feed. Water power was augmented by steam at some sites. In the 21st century, James Cropper plc extended its range of paper and card goods to technical fibres and goods that they export to aerospace and aeronautical industries worldwide.

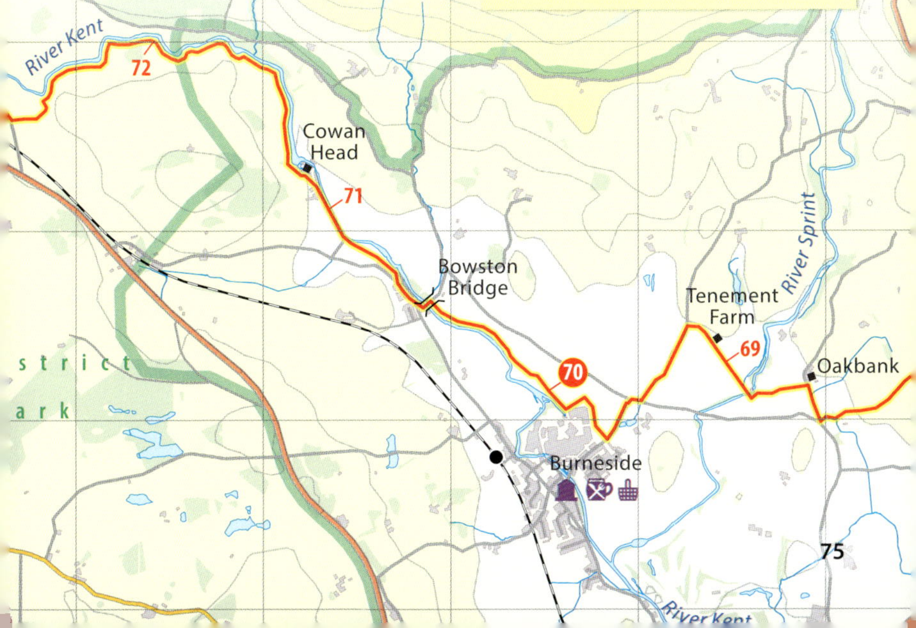

- At the road, turn right to the outskirts of Staveley. Unless visiting the village with its 14th century tower (all that remains of a medieval church), brewery and café, continue the Way.
- After 400 m turn left at Stock Bridge Farm and immediately go left again to pass under the railway at mile 72·9.
- Turn right on a lane and follow the field boundary wall which after 100 m bends left toward a group of houses with a fingerpost. This marks the step-stile that you cross into a garden and driveway past Moss Side farm and houses.
- Leave by the access road, and at the T-junction turn left to cross over the A591. (You could turn right here to reach Staveley station on the Windermere branch line.)
- About 80 m beyond the A591, turn right onto an access road to pass houses on your right (Field Close) and enter a horses field through a gate. Cross the field, channeled between electric fences, and leave by a kissing-gate.
- Go right uphill beside a wood, and after 300 m, descend to turn right along a farm road at mile 73·8. Follow this undulating tarmac road for a mile. Near its high point, pause to enjoy the panorama over the Lakeland fells to the west and the Howgills and Kent valley to the east.
- Descend to a T-junction at mile 74·9 and turn right along this road for 600 m until just before it bends right, where you finally turn left onto a walled track.
- After 300 m the track ends at two field entrances. Go through the metal gate on the right and maintain the same heading on a broad grassy track, later with the wall on your left.
- Pass through a gap in a wall, keeping ahead at first, but the Way soon turns right. Past the conifers on your right, continue to the far end of the plantation over a rugged, rocky section.
- Bear slightly left away from this plantation towards another conifer plantation on your right.
- Continue through a wooden gate and descend to the corner of a stone wall where the grassy track bears right. After another gate, cross a marshy area.

Turn left on a walled track

East over the Howgills and Kent valley from the road (mile 74·3)

- Climb on a vehicle track towards Cragg House Farm at mile 76·5. After the right-hand bend, leave the track and go beside the wall on your right.
- After 250 m the path curves left around the buildings. Go through gates and pass to the right of the buildings.
- At the road, turn right past Outrun Nook farmhouse and go through a gate. Turn left across the cattle grid at the sign for Hagg End and Grandsire Barn: Grandsire is the hill to your right. A prominent LDNP green sign guides you diagonally right among the buildings.
- Afterwards, join a path that climbs to and through open grazing land, past a marshy area on the right. Approaching the crest of the hill, enjoy a glorious panorama of Lake District fells. In clear weather you may even glimpse Scafell Pike to the north-west: at 978 m (3209 ft) it's England's highest mountain.

Heading to Outrun Nook, briefly to join the road

- The descent towards Cleabarrow is across boggy ground featuring lots of exclosures – square timber protected spaces for young shrubs and trees.
- Pass through an open gateway and descend across fields and a stream to pick up a rough vehicle truck which becomes increasingly rocky lower down. Follow it all the way to the fingerpost 'Cleabarrow 1/2 mile' where you turn back sharp left on yourself to head south (mile 77·9).
- Descend past a large pond and follow the lane which, lower down, becomes a tarmac private road that bears left towards the B5284.

Large pond at mile 78·2

Tarmac drive signed for Low Cleabarrow

- Just short of the road, turn right to join the enclosed roadside path just above it. After 130 m turn right up a tarmac drive signed for Low Cleabarrow.
- Before you reach the Business Centre buildings, look for the fingerpost turning you left through a gate and down a field-edge path: descend to another gate, then climb uphill among mature trees.
- Descend to cross Lickbarrow Road at mile 78·9 and go through a gate to enter the lane on the Matson Ground estate. Pass a large pond on your right, rich in wildfowl, and bear left at its end.
- Go through a gate to a track behind the hedge, then cross a field by another gate and pass Brantfell Farm on the left. Descend the path to a huge spreading oak where Lake Windermere finally comes into view.
- Go through a gate and head downhill on a gravelled path to reach a horse-chestnut tree. The stone bench marking the end of the Way matches the one in Ilkley.
- Exit by the gate to Brantfell Road and descend to the streets of Bowness, the lake shore and your accommodation: see page 80.
- If you need to reach Windermere Bus/Rail Interchange quickly, descend to St Martin's Church for a 10-minute journey by Stagecoach bus 599. Some purists may prefer to walk the further 1·7 miles. We recommend the route shown in orange on our online route map: see page 87.

Congratulations on completing the Dales Way.

Harbour view, Bowness-on-Windermere

East over Bowness from the air

Bowness-on-Windermere

Bowness is much older than the settlement around Windermere station, to its north. Both grew after the railway arrived in 1847, and nowadays they have almost merged. Although Bowness looks like a Victorian resort, its origins stem from a much older fishing village. The narrow streets around St Martin's Church hint at how it may have looked two centuries ago.

St Martin's was consecrated in 1483, replacing a much earlier church (1203) destroyed by fire in 1480. Over the centuries, many changes were made, notably the 1870-71 restoration. Its fine stained glass includes a magnificent east window.

Bowness is Cumbria's most visited destination, being the easiest place for visitors to view a lake and distant mountains while enjoying food, drink, shops and hotels. Its residents number about 4000, but the town receives a high proportion of the Lake District's annual 12 million visitors. On summer weekends it can seem saturated with people.

The World of Beatrix Potter celebrates the best-selling children's author Beatrix Potter (1866-1943). She was a talented writer, artist and businesswoman who in 1903 made Peter Rabbit the world's first licensed character. Her later work focused on farming and conservation in the Lake District.

Ferries have plied on Lake Windermere for over 500 years and you can choose from many daily departures, year-round. To return home from Bowness, the bus leaves from the Promenade or St Martin's for Windermere bus/rail station.

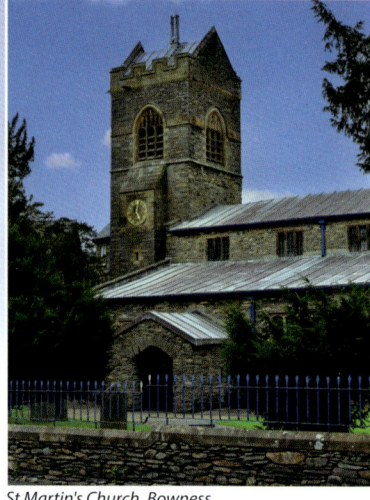
St Martin's Church, Bowness

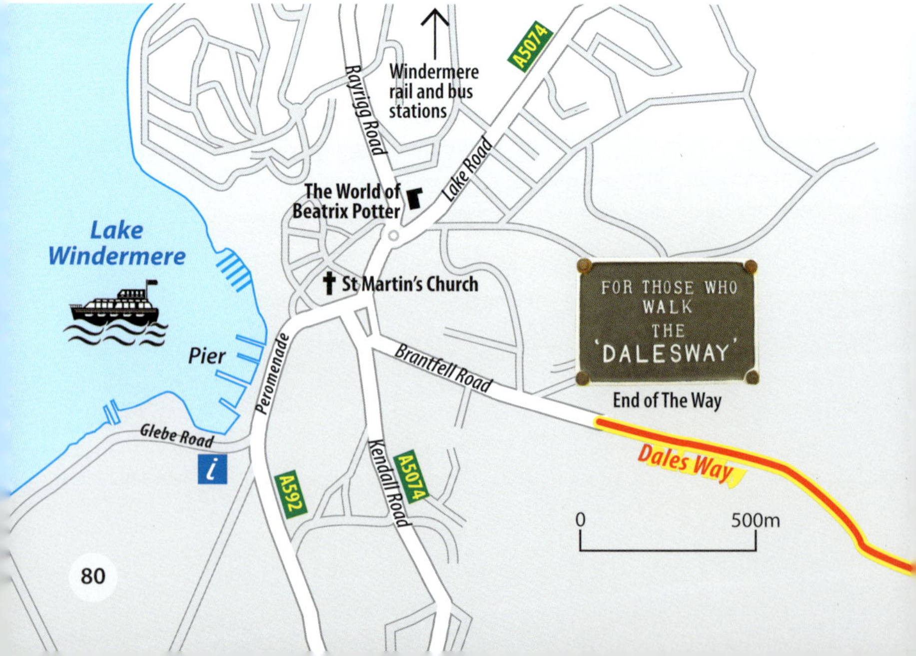

4 Watershed Alternatives   82 83

Distance 9·2 miles 14·8 km (end-to-end: extra distance to rejoin the Way)
Terrain good going underfoot on lanes, bridleways and a drove road, with few boggy bits; 1·7 miles (2·7 km) of minor public road to finish
Grade steep ascent at first, then gradual descent; gentler gradients over Wold Fell (over 500 m/1800 ft); mainly level around Great Knoutberry, then steep descent on road, steeper below Dent Station
Summary these routes create great options for walkers to diverge from the main Way, with wide, lofty views from higher ground; pass Dent Station 1 km before the end, or use the railway to open up fresh options

| 0·0 | 3·7 | | 1·8 | | 3·7 | 9·2 |
| Cam Houses | 5·9 | Newby Head Gate | 2·9 | Arten Gill Moss | 5·9 | Lea Yeat |

To keep the Watershed Alternative options fully open, plan your accommodation accordingly: see pages 14-16. After you've started from Cam Houses, you have choice points at Newby Head Gate and Arten Gill Moss. Normally you can descend to resume the Way from either. These routes follow such well-defined paths and tracks that, even in low cloud or mist, navigation is unlikely to be challenging.

1 Cam Houses to Newby Head Gate

- At Cam Houses (mile 36·4), turn right up the unsigned farm access road (before the metal exit gate with Dales Way fingerpost). Climb steeply uphill on this, following its bend right to reach the T-junction with Cam High Road after 700 m.
- Turn right, still climbing – but more gently. After a further 700 m, reach a junction at Cold Keld Gate (altitude 550 m, comparable with the summit on Wold Fell). Go past a large cattle grid and two gates to the fingerpost at the junction between Pennine Way and Bridleway.
- Go through the gate signed 'Snaizeholme Estate' to follow the grassy, rocky bridleway that curves left before settling into a westerly direction. At first, the terrain is fairly flat, then it starts a long descent through a gate in the stone wall at Gavel Gap after about 1 km.
- Here you join the Ribble Way, which descends in sweeping curves sometimes following streams and passing peat hags, always on a well defined track but boggy in places.
- Descend to the ford across Long Gill and climb again on a spur before swinging right to meet the B6255. The bridleway sign sends you across the road immediately, or take a 40-metre right-left dogleg using the B6255 to keep your feet dry.

South-west across the Long Gill ford to Ingleborough

Pennine Bridleway gate and fingerpost

- Continue west on the minor road for 470 m to reach your first choice point. To rejoin the Dales Way at mile 41·8, keep straight on for a further 500 m and skip to page 55 bullet 6. Do not make this choice unless the public road below Dent Head Viaduct is open to pedestrians.

- Otherwise, turn right through the Pennine Bridleway double gate with fingerpost 'Arten Gill Moss 1¾ miles'.

2 Newby Head Gate to Arten Gill Moss (& descent to Stone House)

- Climb on a broad stony track that becomes grassier as it approaches a gate on the shoulder of Wold Fell. Look behind you for more views of Ingleborough.
- After the gate, the track levels out and goes through a field where cattle may be grazing. Those in the photo on page 82 evoke the name of the drove road that you follow later: Galloway Gate.
- A further gate leads to a narrow path that climbs through sheep grazing to a height of over 550 m. Start to enjoy wide open views ahead to Dentdale.
- A gentle descent follows, veering right beside a stone wall After a final short ascent to a wooden gate, go through the wall to a four-way fingerpost, your next choice point. To continue at high-level on the drove road, skip to page 85.

South-west from the stony track, towards Ingleborough

- To descend to rejoin the Dales Way, instead turn left beside the next stone wall, staying on the Pennine Bridleway for 1·4 miles/2·2 km, following Artengill Beck downstream to your left.
- Your first glimpse of the magnificent Arten Gill Viaduct is just around the first corner. The track descends steadily through several gates and passes through one of the viaduct arches.
- After 1·4 miles (2·2 km) of descent, exit past Stonehouse Farm on its access road to meet the public road and rejoin the Way at mile 43·7. Cross the river and turn right: for directions, skip to page 57 bullet 2.

East from Stonehouse Farm up to Arten Gill Viaduct

3 Around Great Knoutberry and down to Lea Yeat

West over Dentdale from the drove road

- From the four-way fingerpost, turn right uphill through the metal gate signed for the Coal Road and follow the Galloway Gate drove road for the next 2 miles (3·2 km). At first it climbs, then veers left to contour the shoulder of Great Knoutberry at around 520 m (1700 ft).
- The old drove road offers easy, lofty walking with increasingly fine views, to the left over Arten Gill Viaduct and Dentdale, and later (if it's clear) north-west to the distant Lakeland fells.
- A section between two metal kissing-gates overlooks the sweeping curve of the Settle-Carlisle railway with Dent Station, clearly visible above Dentdale.
- Before descending to the road, look behind you (south-west) for the view below.
- At the final gate, exit onto the Coal Road. Turn left to descend this quiet public road quite steeply, passing Dent Station after 1·1 miles/1·7 km. (Catching a train here opens up several options, including the scenic 10-minute ride to Ribblehead to stay at the Station Inn.)
- Below the station, descend steeply through double bends to a T-junction at Lea Yeat, where you turn left to cross the River Dee.
- At the next road, either turn left for 0·6 miles (900 m) for the Sportsmans Inn, or turn right offroad through a gate to resume the Dales Way at mile 44·7: skip to page 58.

South-west to Ingleborough (distant at left) and Whernside

5 Reference

The Dales Way Association (DWA)
The Dales Way Association is a charitable society open to all who support its objectives. We ask you to consider joining for two reasons: first, the DWA provides an excellent newsletter and the Members Area on its website www.dalesway.org has many downloads including a completion certificate, and hosts a fascinating archive. Second, you will be supporting the body that has helped to develop, promote and maintain the Way.

The DWA was formed in 1991 and has over 200 members, to whom it offers great value: in 2026 its membership fee was still only £6 pa. Find practical advice and information on its site www.dalesway.org. For more, visit the site or email
 info@dalesway.org.

National Parks and useful websites
The two National Parks which dominate the Way are described in panels on pages 20 and 25. The Yorkshire Dales National Park website
www.yorkshiredales.org.uk has a wealth of information, and there is also a separate site on the evolution of the landscape:
 www.outofoblivion.org.uk
For conservation work by the Yorkshire Dales Millennium Trust, see www.ydmt.org. For lots of excellent natural history, see the Wharfedale Naturalists website at
 www.wharfedale-nats.org.uk. For the Grassington Lead Trail, visit bit.ly/RR-GLT. For England's Open Access rights and regulations, visit www.openaccess.gov.uk. Visit Cumbria is an independent guide to Cumbria and the Lakes maintained by Julian Thurgood, richly illustrated with fine photos:
 www.visitcumbria.com.

Accommodation sources and tourism websites
Contact the Youth Hostels Association
 www.yha.org.uk for hostels, camping barns and pods. Bedding is included but you need to bring or hire a towel. YHA membership is not required but in 2026 cost only £20 pa (direct debit) and attracts a 10% discount on all bookings.
For accommodation in the Lake District, visit
 www.visitlakedistrict.com and for Yorkshire go to www.yorkshire.com.

Support services
Companies offering packages including accommodation booking for self-guided Dales Way walkers are listed on our web page at bit.ly/DAW-support. Some include baggage transfer, others treat it as an optional extra and a couple offer baggage transfer alone.

Visitor Information Centres
There are information centres along the route as follows. Some have cafés as well as offering free information, and some are open daily year-round. Out of season, expect restricted opening hours and smaller places may be closed on weekdays and/or Sundays:

Ilkley	01943 436 232
Grassington (YDNP)	01756 751 690
Sedbergh	01539 620 125
Bowness (LDNP)	01539 724 555
Windermere (station)	01539 446 499

Transport
National and local journey planning
 www.traveline.info
Train information and tickets
 www.nationalrail.co.uk
Long distance buses
 www.nationalexpress.com and
 www.stagecoachbus.com
Metro, the West Yorkshire Combined Authority, has a journey planner at
 www.wymetro.com
DalesBus offers year-round routes throughout the Dales with extra services in season (usually Easter to mid-October) and on Sundays and Bank Holidays. Their website provides maps and timetables:
 www.dalesbus.org
Settle-Carlisle Railway:
 settle-carlisle.co.uk

Places along the Way
Our web page bit.ly/DAW-links lists websites with specific details on ten villages and towns along the Way.

Weather
 www.metoffice.gov.uk provides forecasts for Yorkshire & Humber area and Northwest England, with extra information for both National Parks.

Notes for novices
Advice on preparation and gear is offered at *rucsacs.com*: scroll to the foot of the page and click/tap the yellow button.

Maps (printed and online)
The mapping in this guidebook appears also in a handy, rainproof 40-page booklet, the perfect pocket partner: our Dales Way map booklet includes the Link Routes at full scale, and also town plans of Ilkley and Bowness. For more, including sample map pages, visit **bit.ly/DAW-MB**
For a very detailed online route map, visit **www.rucsacs.com/books/daw** and click/tap on the map graphic: zoom in for amazing detail. By 2026, this map had over 217,000 views.

Link Routes
The LDWA (*ldwa.org.uk*) has documented Link Routes for walkers starting from Leeds, Bradford and Harrogate. These are mapped in our map booklet (see above) and by Speakman (see below). We thank John Sparshatt for his GPX files of the Link Routes which we used in our map booklet and online overlay at **bit.ly/DAW-LinkRoutes**

Further reading
Bradshaw, Mike *The Yorkshire Dales* (Slow Travel Guide) Bradt Travel Guides (3rd ed) 2024 978-1-80469-216-5
Organised geographically, this insider guide covers the Yorkshire Dales including Nidderdale AONB, with accommodation, food, wild swimming and Dark Skies.

Budgett, Martin and Megarry, Jacquetta *Friends Way 1* (2022) and *Friends Way 2* (2023) 978-1-913817-06-0 and 978-1-913817-07-7
Two guidebooks that cover George Fox's 1652 journey that led him to found Quakerism and Margaret Fell's journey from teenage bride to mother of Quakerism.

Grogan, Tony and Chris *A Dales High Way Companion* Skyware Press 2018 978-1-911321-00-2
Describes a 90-mile challenging high route launched in 2008, nearly 40 years after the Dales Way that inspired it. The route runs from Saltaire to Appleby-in-Westmorland and a Route Guide is also available from Skyware.

Rhodes, Kate *Bolton Abbey: the Priory Church of St Mary and St Cuthbert* Jarrold Publishing 1990 Out of print but still available online
Booklet (16 pp) with fine photos and detailed history of the priory, including the east wall symbolism and stained glass.

Speakman, Colin *Dales Way: the Complete Guide* Skyware Press (12th ed) 2024 978-1-911321-09-5
Excellent guidebook to the route by the eminent man who devised it. This 12th edition has annotated strip maps (1:25,000, orientation varies) and photos. Speakman also describes the Link Routes in detail (map scale 1: 50,000, orientation varies).

Acknowledgements
The authors warmly thank Martin Budgett for his route research to revise pages 63-67.

Photo credits
We thank for their images: Mike Bell 12u; Martin Budgett 63 (both), 64u; Jan Fielkowski 61l; Brother Lawrence Lew, OP 30; John Mottram/istockphoto 28m; Pippa Rayner/YDMT 27l; pubgallery.co.uk 47u, 50u; Colin Raw/Getty images front cover; Gordon Simm 27u, 27m, 27l (inset), 28l, 29m, 35l; Jonathan Smith/where2walk.co.uk 53 (both); Peter Stott 50l, 52 (both); Tarmac Ltd 22; Julian Thurgood title page, 21, 64l.

We thank **geograph.org.uk** and photographers: Philip Halling 12l; Martin Dawes 77u, 81; John Walton 54. We thank **dreamstime.com** and photographers: Rambling Tog 14, 16, 65l; David Head 18-19, 26l; Mark Graham 20-21; Steve Liptrot 23; Malthe Nebelung 25; Thomas Langlands 26u; Pepperboxdesign 28u; Brett Critchley 29u; Brian Kushner 29l; Photowitch 31l; Drew Gardner 34; S Billingham 40u; Iain Frazer 40l; Kevin Eaves 51u, 69u; JamesElkington6 51l; Berndbrueggemann 55l; Paul Fleet 57u; Peter Jarvis 61u; Tomasz Wozniak 65u; Sueburtonphotography 68u; Iordanis Pallikaras 78l; Alexey Fedorenko 79; Gunold 80.

All 58 remaining images are © Jacquetta Megarry.

Index

A
accommodation 7, 14, 15, 16, 86
B
Barden Bridge, Tower 40, 42
Black Moss Tarn 71
blanket bog 27
Bolton Priory 30-31, 38, 40
Bowness-on-Windermere 4, 7, 14, 15, 18, 36, 78-80, 86
Buckden 7, 15, 17, 48, 49
Burneside 7,12,15, 72, 73
Burnsall 7, 15, 42, 43
C
camping 15, 19
cattle and walkers 11
Cowgill 7, 56
cranesbill 26, 27
Crook of Lune 67, 68
curlew 27
D
Dales Way Association 4, 86
Dent, Dentdale 6, 7, 15, 21, 58, 60, 61, 84, 85
Dent station 6, 8, 17, 85
distances and overnight stops 6-7
dogs 12
F
facilities table 15
farming 24
G
geology and scenery 20-21
Grassington 15, 16, 17, 20, 22, 23, 44, 45, 86
golden plover 27
H
habitats and wildlife 26-9
hay meadow 11, 26
heather 22, 35
hostels 15, 86
Howgill Fells 21, 64, 66, 68, 76
Hubberholme 12, 15, 49-50
I
Ilkley 7, 8, 15, 16, 17, 33, 34-5, 86
Ilkley Moor 20, 21, 26, 34, 35, 86
Information Centres 23, 34, 86
K
Kettlewell 9, 15, 46, 48
kingfisher 29
L
Lake District National Park 25, 75, 86
Lea Yeat Bridge 57, 58, 85
lime kilns 24, 46, 51

limestone, limestone pavement 20, 21, 24, 28, 42, 43, 44, 46, 55, 57, 61
Lincoln's Inn Bridge 14, 15, 65
Link Routes 5, 33-4, 87
M
maps, mapping 10, 33, 87
meadow pipit 26
Millthrop 14, 64
mining 22, 45
N
Notes for novices 5, 87
P
packing checklist 19
Peacock butterfly 27
pronunciation 12
Q
Quakers and Quakerism 32, 38, 64, 65, 73
quarrying 22
R
railways 4, 7, 17, 23, 25, 61, 78, 80, 86
red-breasted merganser 29
red grouse 26
Ribblehead 4, 7, 15, 16, 17, 19, 23, 54, 85
rivers and lakes 28-9
S
Sedbergh 7, 12, 14, 15, 32, 64, 86
Settle-Carlisle railway 4, 17, 23, 55, 85, 86
sheep 12, 18, 24, 25, 28, 61, 64
smartphones 13, 19
Staveley 15, 76
stoat 28
Strid, the 31, 40, 41
Swaledale (sheep) 28
T
Three Peaks 4, 6, 21, 54
tourism 25, 35, 45, 64
transport and travel 17-18, 86
U
upland moor 26
V
viaducts 4, 6, 7, 16, 17, 18-19, 23, 54, 55, 57, 66, 68-9, 84
W
wagtail, grey, pied and yellow 29
water, drinking 16, 19
water mills 75
Watershed Alternatives 5, 7, 8, 10, 54, 55, 57, 81-5
weather 6, 8, 13, 86
Wharfedale 14, 22, 27, 34, 46-9, 86
Y
Yorkshire Dales National Park 20, 38, 44, 86